What's Wrong with the WTO and How to Fix It

What's Wrong Series

What's Wrong with the WTO and How to Fix It

RORDEN WILKINSON

polity

. . . when the founders of the GATT evoked the link between trade, growth and a better life, few could have foreseen such poverty, homelessness and unemployment as the world now knows. Few would have imagined that the exploitation of the world's abundant resources and a prodigious growth in world trade would have seen the gap between rich and poor widening. And few could have anticipated the burden of debt on many poor nations . . . let us resolve to leave no stone unturned in working together to ensure that our shared principles are everywhere translated into reality.

Nelson Mandela speaking at the 50th Anniversary celebrations of the GATT, 19 May 1998

Contents

About the Author

Rorden Wilkinson is Professor of International Political Economy in the School of Social Sciences at the University of Manchester and Research Director of the University's Brooks World Poverty Institute. He was the 2013 recipient of the Johan Skytte Manuscript workshop award for *What's Wrong with the WTO and How to Fix it*. He is the 2014 recipient of the International Studies Association Society for Women in International Political Economy (SWIPE) Mentoring Award. He is a member of the Editorial Board of the international public policy journal *Global Governance*, a fellow of the Royal Society of Arts, and the co-editor, with Thomas G. Weiss, of the Global Institutions series.

Rorden Wilkinson's previous works include *International Organization and Global Governance* (2014), *Trade, Poverty, Development: Getting beyond the WTO's Doha Deadlock* (2013), *The Millennium Development Goals and Beyond: Global Development after 2015* (2012), *Global Governance, Poverty and Inequality* (2010), *The WTO after Hong Kong: Progress in, and prospects for, the Doha Development Agenda* (2007), *Encyclopedia of Governance* (2007; 2 volumes), *The WTO: Crisis and the Governance of Global Trade* (2006), *The Global Governance Reader* (2005), *Global Governance: Critical Perspectives* (2002) *and Multilateralism and the World Trade Organization: The Architecture and Extension of International Trade Regulation* (2000).

Acknowledgements

This book is my attempt to stand back and distinguish the wood of trade politics from the trees. It may well be that my gaze has lifted too far and I am in fact staring out into space. I have accumulated many debts over the years nonetheless, and some of the ideas contained herein have been formulated in conjunction with, or in response to the work of others – though I cannot hold any of those to whom I am indebted responsible if indeed my gaze has wandered too far.

I owe a large debt of thanks to James Scott, a former doctoral student of mine and frequent co-author, who has gone on to illustrate what all advisors know only too well – that our students are often more capable than we are and most likely go on to more illustrious careers. James' imprint looms large on what follows. I have tried to acknowledge this where possible but, given that our working partnership is more than a decade old, omissions of attribution are inevitable.

I also owe a large debt of gratitude to David Hulme, Craig Murphy and Tom Weiss. David's infectious enthusiasm, boundless energy and foresight in seeing issues of global governance as critical to taking forward the global fight against poverty provided me with the inspiration, institutional resources and intellectual space to complete this project. Craig's patience and willingness to entertain all the ideas I have shared with him over the years, while also gently correcting my errors, are traits from which I have benefited in equal measure. Tom's judgement, humility and clear-mindedness have always caused me to reflect on what it is that I am doing. Working with him for more than a decade has been as much a pleasure as it has been fruitful. All three have been important role models, equally as passionate about making the world a better place as I hope I am myself.

This book benefits from the extraordinary generosity of the Johan Skytte foundation and its willingness to fund and convene a workshop in November 2013 to review the penultimate draft of the manuscript. The generosity of the foundation and of Li Bennich-Björkman and Åsa Viksten Strömbom allowed me to invite a group of stellar critics to Uppsala. Their time, interventions and insights were all important in crafting what follows, for which I am very grateful. In this regard, I am grateful to Debapriya Bhattacharya, Manfred Elsig, Erin Hannah, Bernard Hoekman, David Hulme, Faizel Ismail, Scott Kennedy, Quan Li, James Scott, Silke Trommer, Kate Weaver and Tom Weiss. Thanks are also due to Sally Cawood who provided me with first-rate support during the workshop and in revising the text thereafter and to Gabe Siles-Brügge who also read and gave me useful comments on the manuscript.

Many of the ideas contained herein have been tried out on unsuspecting victims. Three in particular warrant mention: Erin Hannah for the many moments of clarity and inspiration our conversations elicited; Faizel Ismail for the benefit of his experience and his generosity in sharing it; and Quan Li for his intellectual curiosity and conceptual clarity. I am also indebted to those representatives of developed, developing and least-developed countries with whom I have spoken over the years. The British Academy, the Nuffield Foundation, the Henry Luce Foundation, the Rory and Elizabeth Brooks Foundation, and the University of Manchester provided funding for discrete aspects of the research out of which this work emerges. Denise Redston has always provided me with first-rate support – as she did in this endeavour – for which I am grateful. I owe thanks also to Julia Brunt, Kat Bethell, Clare Degenhardt, Rowena Harding and Julie

Rafferty for running a well-oiled and highly productive machine at BWPI, and to Miguel Ghannam and Oliver Turner for their assistance with aspects of the data collection. Louise Knight has been the perfect editor; Pascal Porcheron and the rest of the team at Polity have been exemplary; it has been a pleasure to work with them all.

Most of all I am grateful to my family, Claire, Holly and Ewan, without whom I would not have been able to write this book. They carried on regardless, whether I was locked away writing or vacantly pondering, giving me the time and space I needed to finish the manuscript. I am especially grateful to my children, who constantly reassured me that there would be other times to play Lego, 'do' jigsaws, tuck them in at night, and roll around in the autumn leaves.

One final note: during the writing of this book my dear friend and colleague Norman Geras succumbed to cancer (25 August 1943–18 October 2013). Fitting tributes to Norm's intellectual contribution followed his death, appropriately filling the Twitter- and blog spheres as well as the broadsheet media. Not only have these tributes celebrated an extraordinary life, they have introduced Norm's intellectual endeavours to a new generation. Yet, touching as tributes like these are, they can never quite convey the fullness of what one person means to another. Norm was on the committee that appointed me to my first permanent academic position in 1997 and was the first head of department I served under after taking up that post. We were friends from the off. Our offices were next door to one another and the carpet between them worn threadbare. We would spend the start and the end of the day shooting the intellectual, football and any other breeze, and our free time as rivals across the card table, as well as teammates in staff–student football matches, among many other things. After he retired and moved from Manchester to Cambridge I saw him all too infrequently. This was replaced by his presence on Facebook and Twitter and via normblog. To 'see' him every day on my Twitter and Facebook feeds made the loss of a friend as he moved away seem tolerable, but it did not make up for all of the time we spent together or the sadness one feels from the absence of physical presence when a friend dies. The laughter he generated and kindness he radiated will always stay with me. He is sorely missed. My deepest condolences and warmest wishes to Adèle, Sophie and Jenny.

Tables

Abbreviations

BRICS	Brazil, Russia, India, China, South Africa
CAP	Common Agricultural Policy
DDA	Doha Development Agenda
DDG	Deputy Director-General
DG	Director-General
DSM	Dispute Settlement Mechanism
EC	European Community
ECOSOC	United Nations Economic and Social Council
EEC	European Economic Community
EU	European Union
FAO	Food and Agriculture Organization
FOGS	functioning of the GATT system
FOWTO	functioning of the WTO
G110	Group of One Hundred and Ten developing countries
G2	Group of Two (United States and European Union)
G20	Group of Twenty developing countries
G33	Group of Thirty-Three developing countries
G4	Group of Four (India, China, United States and European Union)
G90	Group of Ninety developing countries
GATS	General Agreement on Trade in Services
GATT	General Agreement on Tariffs and Trade
GPA	Government Procurement Agreement
IBRD	International Bank for Reconstruction and Development

ICTSD	International Centre for Trade and Sustainable Development
ILO	International Labour Organization
IMF	International Monetary Fund
ITC	International Trade Centre
ITO	International Trade Organization
LDC	least-developed country
MDGs	Millennium Development Goals
MFA	Multi-Fibre Arrangement
MFN	Most-Favoured Nation
NAFTA	North American Free Trade Agreement
NAMA	non-agricultural market access
NGO	non-governmental organization
NIC	newly industrialized country
OECD	Organization for Economic Co-operation and Development
SSM	Special Safeguard Mechanism
TNC	Trade Negotiations Committee
TPP	Trans-Pacific Partnership
TPRM	Trade Policy Review Mechanism
TRIMs	Agreement on Trade Related Investment Measures
TRIPs	Agreement on Trade Related Intellectual Property Rights
TTIP	Transatlantic Trade and Investment Partnership
UN	United Nations
UNCTAD	United Nations Conference on Trade and Development
UNCTE	United Nations Conference on Trade and Employment
UNIDO	United Nations Industrial Development Organization
USTR	United States Trade Representative
WEF	World Economic Forum
WEO	World Economic Organization

WHO	World Health Organization
WIPO	World Intellectual Property Organization
WSF	World Social Forum
WTO	World Trade Organization
YAP	Youth Ambassador Programme

Introduction: Starting from here

As I write this book new trade initiatives are being negotiated in the Asia Pacific – in the form of the Trans-Pacific Partnership agreement (TPP) – and the North Atlantic – by way of a trade and investment agreement between the European Union and the United States known as the Transatlantic Trade and Investment partnership (TTIP). Despite noted controversies in which these negotiations have occasionally become mired – not least the Edward Snowden whistle-blowing affair and the October 2013 US government 'shutdown' (see Luce, 2013) – and the 'successful' conclusion of the World Trade Organization's (WTO) December 2013 Bali ministerial conference, much of the commentary in academic journals and the broadsheet media has heralded these mega-regional endeavours as either (and sometimes both) a breakthrough in a global trade politics that has been encased in deadlock since the WTO's Doha round stuttered to a halt in July 2006, or else as a threat to the very existence of the multilateral trading system itself (*Guardian*, 2013; Flowers, 2013). The agreement of a small package of measures covering three broad areas (trade facilitation, agriculture and special and differential treatment for least-developed countries) at the Bali conference has done little to temper these binary perceptions (see Barysch and Heise, 2014; Alden, 2013).

At one level, it matters not that these views are the latest instalment in a cycle of 'received' wisdom about the multilateral trading system that has been heard many times before and which continues to dog the post-Bali WTO (see Lamy, 2013). At another level, they illustrate much that is wrong with the way we think about global trade. They are despairing nonetheless. These views are despairing because they take the Pacific and Atlantic negotiations as proxies for something to which they do not actually relate. In the more optimistic version, the prospect of either a TPP or TTIP – irrespective of whether they are likely to be concluded – is celebrated more out of a relief that trade talks actually seem to be occurring than because of a genuine desire to applaud the positive contributions that each agreement might make to global prosperity (if indeed trade agreements make any difference at all – see Rose, 2004; and Bagwell and Staiger, 2002 for contrasting views). Whereas the more pessimistic variant suggests that the Pacific and Atlantic negotiations provide further evidence of the slow but certain demise of the multilateral trading system. And it speaks more to a familiar way of talking and thinking about trade politics – that any political development other than forward movement in a WTO trade round must be a threat to the wider system – than it does to clear evidence that a causal relationship exists between the rise of regional arrangements and the downfall of that system.

What is particularly despairing is that both of these views encourage us to seek quick fixes to the ills of the multilateral trading system in a way that privileges expediency over contemplation and root-and-branch reform. Rather than encouraging us to stand back and ask 'just what is wrong with the way we organize global trade?' and come up with measured responses based on serious reflection and debate, we are compelled by both views to get the system working, to do so quickly and at almost any cost. Those who celebrate the TPP and TTIP inevitably underline the role that these mega-regional agreements can have as stepping stones to system-wide liberalization while at the same time cautioning of the importance of not losing sight of the multilateral game and encouraging us to redouble our efforts to get the Doha round moving building on the momentum the Bali ministerial has generated. Likewise, more pessimistic accounts of the rise of regional initiatives point to the necessity of concerted and continued action on the multilateral front, lest the system fall into atrophy.

Yet, we know that getting the system working by putting into place short-term measures at successive crisis points across the history of the multilateral trading system has done little for its smooth functioning or to ensure that it acts as a mechanism for promoting trade-led growth and prosperity for all (see Wilkinson, 2006a). We persist nonetheless. This is akin to George Orwell's famous quip that 'we are all capable of believing things which we *know* to be untrue' but acting as if they were regardless (1946). As Orwell remarked '[t]o see what is in front of one's nose needs a constant struggle'. We seem determined to eschew that struggle. We know better; we know that we should look up, 'see' and think harder about how to govern global trade so that it serves our collective interests better; but we do not. Instead, we trot out the same tired and hackneyed 'commonsense' that we have since before the system was created whenever we talk about trade and fall back on the same old tired solutions when the system does not function as we imagine it should.

It is not just debate about the threat or not of regional initiatives, or our rush to tinker with a system whose problems we seldom stand back and dwell upon that is frustrating. Equally problematic is the way that any potentially positive movement forward in WTO politics is set up to fail. This is the case with the election of a new WTO Director-General (DG) as it is in the debate that unfolds ahead of the organization's biennial ministerial conference. In both cases, hope soon gives way to despair as the cold light of national interests and entrenched positions come into focus, leaving the capacity of successive DGs to make a difference nullified and the average likely outcome of a ministerial conference practically nil or else the agreement reached rendered impracticable from the off – to which the elections of Mike

Moore (1999–2002), Supachai Panitchpakdi (2002–5), Pascal Lamy (2005–13) and Roberto Carvalho de Azevêdo (2013–), and ministerial circuses that have been Geneva (1998), Seattle (1999), Cancún (2003), Hong Kong (2005), Geneva again (2009, 2011) and Bali (2013), amply testify. We choose to persevere nonetheless.

Problematic still is the way that 'threats' to the multilateral trading system are crafted around the 'rise' of new powers. This is equally the case with the rise, during the 1960s, of a reconstructing Europe, of Japan in the 1970s and 1980s, and China since (see Krause, 1963; Evans, 1971; Mansfield, 1989; Scott and Wilkinson, 2013a). What has often started out as a uniquely US debate played out periodically whenever challenges to American supremacy are perceived – in global trade as well as elsewhere – has subsequently spread to draw other countries and commentators into the speculation and hyperbole that accompanies successive 'waves' of 'rising' powers. It is rare, for instance, to find a contemporary high-level policy discussion anywhere in the world – including those attended by foreign visitors in China – that does not fall at some level back on debating China's rise/threat/challenge/intentions and/or that of the other major BRICS (Brazil, Russia, India, China, South Africa) powers. This was also the case during the 1980s with regard to Japan and the 1960s and 1970s with regard to the European Economic Community (EEC).

What is despairing about the way rising threats are constructed is their use as a means of smuggling in and legitimizing discriminatory measures into debates about trade. What is also unique about this kind of politics is the way that it is connected to the pursuit of grand trade measures – often in the form of mega-regional initiatives – designed, in part, to gain leverage over (or at worst isolate) third-party states. During the Uruguay round (1986–94) the negotiation of the North American Free Trade Agreement (NAFTA) was intended, in part, to be a leveraging device *vis-à-vis* the EEC and to a lesser extent Japan (see, for instance, Bhagwati,

1993). Likewise, both the TPP and TTIP negotiations are seen as ways of isolating and undermining the potential might (collective or otherwise) of the BRICS in the Doha round (see, for example, Pilling, 2011; Lehmann, 2013). The current plurilateral renaissance in the WTO is similarly constructed.

The point here is that all too often our commentary on the state of the round and on the WTO more broadly unfolds in ways that are knowable, circular and ultimately hopeless, whether they speak to the examples above or are manifest elsewhere. It is no longer sufficient simply to show that the logic and reality of these and other arguments about trade are flawed. We have to draw a line in the sand and find ways of moving beyond these familiar arguments wherein almost nothing new is offered and towards those which are better able to contribute to a world order wherein enduring poverty, destitution, easily curable disease, insecurity, un- and under-employment cease to be the life experiences of most of the planet's population. We need to stand back and observe the problems of the WTO in a longer and wider view and be willing to think critically about what we think we know to be 'true' about the format and consequences of the way we govern trade; and we need to think about wider social values to which we ought to attach global trade governance rather than come up with quick fixes when we consider what we should do now – whether plurilateral, repackaged aid (for trade) or otherwise.

Yet, we have become blinded by a debate that is *always* waged as if the very existence of the multilateral trading system were at risk and which is acutely and unnecessarily pressured as a consequence. Former WTO DG Pascal Lamy's (2013) account of threats to the multilateral trading system in the wake of the agreement of the Bali package is one such example. As a result we fail really to see that: (i) the form of trade governance that so many of us worry about has been applied only selectively to the liberalization of markets of economic interest to the major trading powers while at the same time restricting the capacity of smaller, less able developing states to develop their commercial advantages; and (ii) the circular ways we talk about trade *reinforce* rather than attenuate that situation. We fail to see what is going on because to do so would require us to acknowledge that the system is broken and failing to deliver trade gains for all, which would in turn threaten to undermine the very argument for freer trade.

Acknowledging that the system is fundamentally broken and that we need a new way of governing global trade is precisely what we should do. We would not expect a large corporation, public or private institution, or government to be run well in the absence of effective management, nor would we expect such an absence to ensure that it was free of unfair gain, advantage or corruption. So why would we eschew these expectations when it comes to managing the global economy and the way we govern trade? Simply put, we need a world trade organization – without one we cannot hope to help secure the kind of growth needed to attenuate global asymmetries in power, income, wealth and life experiences or to mitigate the accrual of unfair gain and advantage – but we need it to be organized differently and to adopt a different mechanism for generating commercial opportunities for all. We need a different set of values to which it speaks and upon which it is anchored. Moreover, we need to change the way we think and talk about trade. We need to disavow ourselves of the idea that trade can be separated from other areas of economic and social life – as we have falsely imagined it can – and that the WTO is not a development organization. We need to begin to think about global governance generally as well as trade governance more specifically in more coherent and joined-up ways eschewing our overly myopic approach to organizing global life (see Weiss and Wilkinson, 2014). Despite the 'successes' of Bali, we need to do all of this soon, otherwise the WTO and the Doha round will continue to stutter along in a business-as-usual fashion and, in so doing, be confined to further irrelevance. And we need to recognize that we do ourselves a disservice in rendering moribund an institution that *could* help make a dramatic difference where it is needed most.

Our first act ought to be to divorce ourselves from ideas of blame about who is at fault for the state we are in. More often than not these ideas of who is to blame are played out in repeat performances of a largely imagined and rather tired 'North–South theatre' (Weiss, 2012b: 119–21; Turner, 2013: 1201–3) – the *New York Times* editorial board's assertion (2013) that the Doha round has been 'stymied largely because of disagreements between industrialized economies like the United States and European Union on the one hand and developing countries like China and India on the other' is a good example. In truth we are all at fault. We have all been complicit in the system's operation – whether we have actually been at the trade negotiating coalface, simply stood outside as commentators, or squirrelled away as knowledgeable but nonetheless silent bystanders; and we have all been complicit in the system's perpetuation by engaging in a politics that produces, at best, only piecemeal solutions to problems perceived but which nonetheless preserves a form of governance that enables the leading industrial states to protect their markets against cheaper imports, thus reducing the export opportunities of their poorer, less-developed counterparts. Thus we should resist the temptation to issue proclamations such as Jagdish Bhagwati's assertion that '[t]he multilateral trading system is dead and the Doha Round is in trouble largely because of lack of US leadership' (CUTS, 2013). We should resist these because, although they are designed to get the United States back to the negotiating table, they are counterproductive, generate hostility and entrench positions further. Once we have extracted ourselves from the proclivity to blame, we can begin to work on overhauling a system that Thomas Pogge argues 'greatly aggravates severe poverty in less-developed countries' (Pogge, 2010: 20). If we do not, pursuing questions of who *really* is to blame will do little more than ensure future negotiations flounder in the way that their predecessors have.

National trade negotiators inevitably pursue trade openings (and closings) that speak to those interests – primarily large corporate lobbies or at least what they imagine big business will want – that have the biggest voice in determining domestic commercial policy. 'Good' negotiators give away as little as possible for as much as they can get. As citizens of nation-states we would expect nothing else from our governments. Where we have erred is in allowing the pursuit of national economic interest to occur without ensuring that our responsibilities to others as well as the planet as a whole are also front and centre. These are responsibilities not only to the global environment – the diverse eco- and bio-systems that are conjured up when we talk about 'planetary' responsibility – but also the majority of the world's population that are the 'global left behind' (see Hulme and Turner, 2014). In large measure, these people live in those developing and least-developed countries that are, and have consistently been, frozen out of global trade negotiations because their contribution to world trade is so small that they are deemed to be unworthy of a seat at the table. Yet, it is they that would benefit most from a system that took responsibilities as seriously as it does the pursuit of the national gain of the developed world.

These responsibilities are at least three-fold, all of which matter in this book albeit the third is perhaps the most visible in the analysis that follows. First, as a global collective we should seek to construct and confine our activity on this planet to forms of production and consumption that have, at the very least, a minimal negative impact on the global eco-system. Second, we should constantly reflect on the way we behave and the systems of governance that give rise to that behaviour with a view to continual refinement so that we safeguard life on this planet in all its forms and secure the earth's resources for future generations. Third, we should seek to attenuate any negative circumstances that have arisen from the forms of governance we have put in place, particularly those that continue to serve as frameworks for organizing global life. In this way, 'we' as citizens of those states that have benefited from the construction of forms of global economic governance that have delivered not only disproportionate gains, but advantages that have been at the expense of poor countries, have a duty to offer assistance designed to ameliorate destitution as well as to correct for past injustices. That we should take these responsibilities seriously goes without saying. Acknowledging that we have both the material capabilities and technological capacity to make a dramatic difference to the lives of the global left behind requires more widespread acknowledgement – the devastating impact of the recent financial crisis on the lives of the already vulnerable in the industrial world notwithstanding.

The task of understanding how we can change what we have done and how our responsibilities can become a fruitful corner-stone of a new multilateral trading system begins in Chapter 4. To understand how we have erred so much we need to explore a little of the consequences of the way we have organized trade, why we have persisted with a form of trade governance that is deeply problematic and fundamentally flawed, and what we think it is that we have been – and are – doing.

About the book

More than a decade ago, in his assessment of the most commonly touted charges against the WTO, philosopher Peter Singer warned that:

> ... genuine open-minded exploration of the crucial and difficult issues arising from globalization is losing out to partisan polemics, long in rhetoric and thin in substance, with each side speaking only to its own supporters who already know who the saints and the sinners are. (Singer, 2004: 55; also 51–105)

Few have heeded Singer's advice. This book tries to be different. It aims to move beyond the commonsense construction of 'supporters' and 'opponents' of free trade entrenched in ever more heavily fortified positions generating proclamations that speak to their congregations rather than which seek to engage their opponents in genuine debate. The book is not intended to be an emphatic rebuttal of existing wisdom or a heavily scholarly corrective to dominant ways of thinking about trade. Nor is it intended to be a disquisition on cause and effect in multilateral trade governance that will be read by scant few. Rather, it is designed to advance an argument seldom heard in debate about the WTO and international trade – that we need to take the system apart and put it back together in a way that enables tradeled growth to occur but that does so in a manner that offers an equity of opportunity across the board and substantial corrective action for those who have been negatively affected by the system's past functioning. Put another way, we need a world trade organization; but we do not need one that functions in the way it currently does.

We underestimate the extent to which competing positions are entrenched and the task of overcoming the divides that lie between them at our peril. So compelling is their camouflage that we seldom notice from where sticks are being thrown, let alone understand the driving motivations. We should resist the temptation to be drawn in by what seem to be easily consumable nuggets of commonsense but which are in fact little more than bombastic journalistic turns of phrase designed to garner support or sell more newspapers than genuine attempts at advancing debate. Thomas Friedman's (1999) claim that there is little 'more ridiculous' than the 'Noah's ark of flat-earth advocates, protectionist trade unions and yuppies looking for their 1960s' fix' protesting during the WTO's 1999 ministerial conference, and Vandana Shiva's ([2000] 2006: 280) admonishment of the WTO's 'rules of robbery, camouflaged by arithmetic and legalese' are good examples of pithy turns of phrase that are ultimately destructive.

I make no claim to having all of the answers about what we should do. I am nonetheless sufficiently tired of hearing and reading the same old expedience versus alarmist commentary, 'bound to fail' ways of talking, 'next threat' spotting pastimes and 'business trumps morality' statements that continue to underpin calls for a continuation of multilateral trade liberalization as usual. It is time that we thought outside the box and organized global trade – and the rest of the way we order life on this planet – differently. At the same time we should shake ourselves from our feverish obsession with pressing forward with every greater liberalization in new areas without first attending to the restrictions and structural problems that affect those least able to take advantages of frontier-sector opportunities, or worse, stand back while our business-as-usual approach to trade governance further entrenches the misery of the many.

The purpose of this book is to shine a light on what we have been doing wrong as well as to offer pointers that may help us do things differently. Irrespective of whether my arguments for a fundamentally reformed system are compelling or not we need to start engaging in a conversation that produces a better way forward and which connects the governance of global trade up with the realization of certain progressive social goods. A good place to start is by asking questions about how and why we have got to where we are. To do this we need to ask questions about:

(i)   What have been the consequences of governing trade in the way that we do?
(ii)   Why have we governed trade in this fashion?
(iii) Why do we think and talk about trade in circular and uncritical ways?
(iv)   How can we think differently?
(v)   What would a more progressive system look like?
(vi)   How can we get from where we are to where we should be going?

It is these questions that motivate what follows, structuring each of the chapters hereafter and which together present the argument of the book.

Before we begin, it is important to spell out what this book is *not* about. The book does not offer a 'nuts and bolts' guide to the WTO, though I have tried to write, in as far as it is possible, in an accessible way that does not presume too great a familiarity with the topic. Filling the pages that follow with basic facts and descriptions would act as a distraction to the development of the argument, particularly as good introductory works on the WTO exist elsewhere (for instance Hoekman, 2014; and Hoekman and Mavroidis, 2007). Nor do I treat the WTO as a monolithic – indeed leviathan-esque – institution, a single and dominant agent operating functionally in accordance with a pre-prescribed neoliberal logic (such as, for instance, Peet, 2009). Certainly, I am critical of the WTO – and the global economic order to which its functioning has helped give rise – and the consequences of its deployment and the functioning it has produced. Yet what often fells critical accounts of the WTO is the presentation of the institution as a dark, foreboding and unchecked bureaucracy operating on whim and will alone.

In reality there are a number of WTOs – distinct personalities that need specifying when points are being unpacked and claims being made. The first is an organization comprising a secretariat and director-general. The second is body of international law and a quasi-juridical apparatus designed to interpret and enforce that law. The third is a collection of member states – numbering 160, following the acceptance of Yemen's accession at the December 2013 Bali ministerial conference – that are the principal actors in this multilateral tale and who are authoritative in that they agree to the negotiation of forms of trade regulation and the primary parties bound by that regulation (albeit to varying degrees). The fourth is a collection of private actors who play a role in the governance of global trade – law firms, public intellectuals, think tanks and non-governmental organizations – by attempting to shape the contours of debate and the negotiating positions of states as well as advance their own special interests (see Tussie, 2009). Each one of these personalities looms large at given moments, though none more prominently than the member states. Throughout, my aim is to identify clearly just which WTO I have in mind when I am developing an aspect of the argument that follows.

That said, despite my effort to write this book in an accessible fashion and designed for a broad, informed, interested but not necessarily intimately familiar audience of scholars, practitioners, policymakers and lay parties, what follows is nonetheless involved and at times finitely engaged. Trade and its governance is a jargon-laden field and a certain complexity cannot be avoided when engaging on that terrain. For ease of understanding my argument is as follows:

(1) Trade governance in the post-Second World War era has generated a series of asymmetrical bargains that have offered developed countries greater economic advantages than their developing counterparts – advantages which, in turn, have contributed to the growing global gap between those who have and those who do not;

(2) These asymmetrical bargains have come about because we have installed competitive negotiating among unequals as the machinery of trade governance;

(3) We have failed to fully comprehend or accept this state of affairs because we are blinded by a way of talking about trade that treats free trade and the WTO as synonyms (when they are not) and which precludes progressive debate;

(4) The vast majority of our suggestions for, and attempts to, reform the multilateral trading system have the effect of *reinforcing* rather than attenuating the current state of affairs;

(5) A thoroughly reformed WTO needs to be reoriented so

that the realization of global social goods are the priority and trade liberalization and commercial regulation are the machinery by which they are achieved (rather than the other way around); and

(6) Getting from here to there requires a clear and consistent plan that uses what we currently have as a leveraging device but which resists falling back on existing ways of operating.

Starting a different kind of conversation

The argument that follows develops in two parts with each of the chapters contained therein unfolding around the six questions outlined above. The first part explores the problems with multilateral trade governance as currently conceived. Its purpose is to peel back the covers of what we think we 'see' to reveal what lies beneath. In Chapter 1, the book probes the very design of the system of trade governance we currently have. Its purpose is to dislocate the idea of post-war multilateral trade liberalization from its reality, illustrating that what has evolved has been a form of trade governance that favours the few over the many. In Chapter 2, the book examines the mechanism by which post-war liberalization has been conducted. Here the purpose is to unpick the notion that it is any longer useful to expect that the self-stated aims of the multilateral trading system can be delivered through a system of bargaining that pitches states of dramatically different capabilities against one another and does so in the context of an institutional environment that further exacerbates these inequalities. Chapter 3 focuses on the commentary that surrounds trade and the WTO. Here, the aim is to demonstrate how the way that we talk about trade compounds matters, heightening tensions over negotiations and adding to a broader sense of stasis, while at the same time locking us into path-dependent ways of thinking about reform of the WTO.

The second part of the book considers how all of the problems identified with WTO's design and application as well as the commonsense wisdom that circulates about trade can be circumscribed and a new more progressive and socially beneficial institution created. In Chapter 4, the book asks 'what really constitutes reform of the WTO?' cautioning against measures that will perpetuate rather than attenuate the problems in the system's functioning. Here the aim is to embark on a more fundamental process of reflection on the value of the multilateral trading system that moves beyond merely tinkering at the margins, that reconnects the governance of global trade with progressive social values, and which moves beyond unhelpful debate about the WTO's role – or not – as a development organization. In Chapter 5, the book asks how trade might be organized so that it produces gains that are more equitable and congruous with the vast majority of members' development needs, while at the same time not eschewing the political realities and economic necessities of the WTO's leading industrial members. The key to this chapter is recognizing that a wholesale change in the organizing mechanisms and principles of global trade is required, and that what is required is an institution that functions much more like a national department of trade and industry. In Chapter 6, the book sets out a roadmap of how we get from the unsatisfactory state of affairs we are in to a more progressive form of governance. Here the book strips away the confines of existing debate, opening up a space that is better able to reflect on the future and value of the multilateral trading system; and it explores how the WTO's existing machinery can be used as a vehicle for change. The book draws to a close underlining the dangers we face if we choose not to move from the divisive moment we are in to a new more fruitful trade politics and system of governance, what this means for the way we think about the global institutions we have, and why (and how) we need to seize the opportunity for change.

Part I

Problems

CHAPTER ONE

Why we govern trade in the way that we do

While Peter Singer reminds us that it is not possible to prove that the liberalization pursued under the GATT/WTO has made 'the rich richer and the poor poorer' (Singer, 2004: 91), the form of trade governance that we currently have – and with which we have persisted in the post-Second World War era – has presided over the exacerbation of precariousness in the poorest parts of the world and has undergone little more than a rearranging of the furniture reform-wise since it was established. This form of trade governance has produced a pattern of liberalization that has accorded the lion's share of trade opportunities to the leading industrial states, offered others limited prospects, and for others still excluded them from openings in key economic sectors inhibiting their capacity to take advantage of the opportunities that trade-led growth could bring. As Jennifer Clapp and Kim Burnett (Clapp and Burnett, 2014: 79) put it:

> Despite being shaped by ideas that trade liberalization will bring benefits to all, the regime in practice has locked in an imbalanced set of rules and practices that have contributed to the vulnerability in the world's poorest countries. This system has contributed to hunger and poverty, especially in a world that is facing ongoing volatility in food prices.

Exaggerated claims concerning the value of the benefits from GATT/WTO negotiations notwithstanding (see Scott and Wilkinson, 2011; Scott, 2008; Panagariya, 1999; Whalley, 2000), the outcome of successive trade rounds has produced neither significant value nor opportunity for the broad swathe of non-industrial states. As Nelson Mandela (1998) put it, 'the extent to which all parties have benefited [from international trade] has depended on the circumstances in which [trade has] taken place'.

The paradox here is that our belief in the inalienable good of freer trade has been such that we have seldom raised questions about the way we have pursued liberalization. What we have done instead is to fixate on applying modest advances designed to overcome moments of blockage and intransigence. In so doing, we have failed to see that the system is not only broken but it is complicit in the perpetuation of this sorry state of affairs. The problem – which we need to recognize and move quickly away from – is that what has passed for multilateral liberalization under the GATT/WTO has been treated, rather uncritically, as a synonym for free or freer trade, and not understood as a managed form of regulation strategically applied in pursuit of the specific and particular interests of the leading industrial states (Wilkinson, 2011). We need to undo this simple association, and to divorce the idea of greater universal prosperity through freer trade from the multilateral means by which we have pursued liberalization in the post-war era.

This point is worth dwelling on for a moment. It is not the idea of freer trade through multilateral means that is necessarily at issue here (though, equally, I am not arguing for unregulated markets – their capacity to work in an equitable fashion is far too limited to justify the omission of a regulatory apparatus designed to constrain some forms of behaviour, mitigate others, banish others still and to assist the poorest and most vulnerable); rather it is the way that this idea has been put into operation – that is, the manner in which liberalization has been pursued and economic openings and forms of protection safeguarded – in the post-Second World War era that is the problem. It is, as the next chapter argues, unimaginable that we would – given carte blanche – construct a fair and equitable system of freer trade on the basis of bargaining among states of vastly different capabilities. Yet this is exactly what we have let happen. It is equally unimaginable that we would withhold trade openings in sectors of key economic importance, principally agriculture, to the poorest producers in the pursuit of a meaningful development agenda – as we have done and are doing in the Doha round (a topic to which we return throughout this book). Moreover, it is difficult to imagine that we would persist with simplistic ideas and quasi-intellectual-cum-metaphorical ways of thinking and talking about trade that obscure what is actually going on if we sat down and seriously thought about the reasons why we think global trade governance might be a good thing in the first place – a topic that Chapter 3 explores. Yet this is exactly what we have done.

Before we can explore how the form of trade governance we currently have acts as a mechanism for distributing commercial opportunities, or the arcane manner in which we have tended to think and talk about trade, we first need to know something about the kind of trade governance that we actually have, how it has evolved, and what the consequences of that evolution have been. This is important not only because it helps uncover why we have persisted with one particular form of trade governance, it also adds substance to the claims of inequity that are the motivations driving the need to build a new global trade order.

The aim of this chapter is to explore the trade governance that we actually have (not the one we might imagine that we do). It begins at the formation of the multilateral trading system, moving through key moments, events, outcomes and decisions before arriving all too briefly at today. Its argument is that like most, but not all, international regimes and institutions the development of the multilateral trading system has been largely in keeping with the ideas and interests that were the alloy out of which it was forged; and it is this narrow and partisan institutional creation and evolution that accounts in large part for the problems we encounter today.

What trade governance we actually have

It is not unreasonable to ask why we govern trade in the way that we do and why we persist with a system that is clearly not delivering meaningful gains to those who need them most. The simple answer is that we govern trade in the way that we do because it is the way that we always have; and we have persisted with it because we treat the existing system as if it were a fact of nature and imagine that it cannot be fundamentally changed. Yet, rather than asking ourselves these questions we have resigned ourselves to carrying on with a system of trade governance that is not perfect but probably the best we think we can imagine; and we have merely tinkered at the margins as a result. In so doing, we have eschewed questions about whether (and how) trade could be governed more efficiently and equitably.

If we were to ask ourselves these questions, we would realize that we govern trade in the way that we do because we have persisted with an *ad hoc* form of liberalization that was put in place in an attempt to salvage something from a complex and protracted, but ultimately unsuccessful set of post-war trade negotiations; and because the result of that salvage operation spoke more pointedly to the economic interests of the leading powers at that time. This system has, in turn, survived precisely because it has continued to speak to a narrow set of commercial imperatives as well as through familiarity and habit. There were moments when its very existence was threatened, but challenges to its supremacy as the primary means of governing trade – most notably in the form of United Nations Conference on Trade and Development (UNCTAD, see Gardner, 1964) – were successfully countered. What has occurred instead has been a slow process of consolidation and legalization which has resulted in the embedding of a system salvaged from one project and designed for a specific post-war purpose that continues as the foundation around which contemporary trade is governed.

That it is no longer fit for purpose has been obvious for a considerable period of time. The degree of contestation that has developed over the course of consecutive trade rounds – which was present during the first post-war negotiations and has amplified since – provides ample illustration of this. The more visible challenges to contemporary trade governance that have taken place since the WTO was established, most notably during its biennial ministerial conferences, further reinforce the point. That the system needs fundamentally overhauling is equally obvious. Yet, the sunk costs – in terms of the amount of time, effort and energy that have been invested, not to mention the development of trade capacities and the construction of trade missions in Geneva as well as in national capitals designed to deal with the current system – are such that an exercise of the scale required is unappealing. It is nevertheless precisely what we should do. To understand why we should recapture that appeal, it is necessary to establish precisely what the nature of the system of trade governance that we have is as well as to explore what the consequences of its application in the post-Second World War period have been.

The creation and development of the multilateral trading system

As is recounted in most histories of the multilateral trading system, the origins of the WTO lie in the ill-fated wartime and post-war efforts to create an International Trade Organization (ITO) as the third of a triumvirate of institutions designed to manage the global economy – with the other two being the International Monetary Fund (IMF) and what was to become the World Bank. Yet, most of these accounts merely note that the WTO's predecessor, the General Agreement on Tariffs and Trade

(GATT), grew out of designs for an ITO and not the fact that the GATT was actually a response to blockages in the ITO negotiations. It is understanding why this response was necessary that holds the key to appreciating why the GATT developed in the way that it did and why we have the kind of trade governance that we currently have. This, in turn, requires an appreciation of the motivations of the institution's lead architect (the United States), how these motivations (and the interests to which they spoke) were expressed in the GATT's design, and how a multilateral forum (the ITO) proved insufficient and led a mini-lateral gathering (the GATT) to become the primary means of governing global trade. It is to that deeper narrative that we now turn.

By the end of the Second World War, US economic fortunes were almost the mirror opposite of what they had been in the depression of the 1930s. The United States ended the war in a position of unrivalled economic pre-eminence. It was, as Alan Milward (1979: 330) put it, 'inevitable that [US] economic policy ... would be the chief factor in determining the post-war international economy'. He continued, the problem for the United States was no longer one of 'how to share out an inadequate level of income and employment by the cautious regulation of output [as it had been during the depression] but rather how to sustain the economy after the war at the new levels of output which it had attained' (Milward, 1979: 330). By one measure the United States ended the war accounting for approximately one third of total world production and more than 50 per cent of total world output of manufactured goods (Wilcox, 1949a: 10). This, as Clair Wilcox remarked (1949a: 10–11), put the United States in a position to sell 'everything to everybody', while needing to buy very 'little of anything from anybody'.

US pre-eminence did not, however, come without challenges. During the war, economic recovery had been fuelled by strong and stable demand for US products. Much of this demand stemmed from large-scale government contracts for everything from heavy machinery and weaponry to agricultural produce and dried foodstuffs (see Cooke, 2007 for an insightful account). These contracts were designed to support the US war effort as well as to supply the Allied powers with supplies under the Lend-Lease programme (Stettinius, 1944). Once the war was over, this demand evaporated. At home, government contracts for US produce dried up as the economy moved to a peacetime footing; internationally, demand shrunk as the financial circumstances of the Allies worsened with the end of US assistance and other pro-grammes, such as the Canada's provision of mutual aid to Britain and the Commonwealth (see Rooth, 1999). So, while it was the case that the United States ended the war in a position to supply just about anything to anyone, it quickly became clear that few were in a position to buy those goods.

The response of the United States was to pursue a post-war international economic policy that would stimulate demand for its goods overseas and which would, in turn, assist with European reconstruction. Four obstacles need to be overcome for US plans to be effective.[1] First, the spread of depression in the inter-war years had caused many governments to implement trade-restricting and trade-diverting commercial policies in an effort to protect their national economies. Second, high tariff and other barriers lent foreign producers a measure of protec-tion that enabled them to compete with US goods. Third, much of the colonized world was effectively closed to the commercial reach of the United States by imperial preference systems that guaranteed markets for products from the imperial powers and provided them with near exclusive access to vital raw materials. Fourth, and most significantly, the United States needed not only to ensure its goods entered foreign markets as competitively as possible, it also needed to ensure that there was sufficient capac-ity to pay for those goods.

Some of this demand could be stimulated by prising open imperial preference systems. This alone would not, however, have been sufficient. The United States also needed to stimulate demand in its most likely market: Europe. However, in the absence of a reconstruction package, European demand for both capital and consumer goods would have been minimal and certainly not enough to help stave off post-war depression. Moreover, for US producers to take advantage of any European demand, the means by which goods were purchased had to be fully convertible into dollars. The solution was to provide Europe with the wherewithal to purchase US goods through a programme of loans and grants known as Marshall Aid (officially the European Recovery Program) (see Hogan, 1987) and to put into place a mechanism for ensuring currency convertibility (see van Dormael, 1978).

US plans to liberalize trade in the post-war era did, however, have a significant caveat: agriculture. Price deflation during the 1920s and the 1930s had hit the US agricultural sector particularly hard and tariffs, production controls, price-support schemes, import quotas and export subsidies had been put in place in response (Evans, 1971: 61–3, 66–9). Moreover, the strength of the agricultural lobby in key US states made any attempt to pursue liberalization therein unlikely to succeed (Gardner, 1956: 3, 20–1). The result was that while the United States was willing to liberalize trade in those sectors where it could accrue economic gain (and wherein it faced little competition), it was not willing to do the same in areas of political and economic sensitivity. This liberal-mercantilist approach, particularly with regard to agriculture, became a cornerstone of the GATT.

The designs for what would have eventually become the ITO were what Robert Hudec (1990: 10) described as a résumé of ideas developed across myriad inter-war and wartime gatherings. Yet, in contrast to designs for the financial (IMF) and monetary (World Bank) aspects of the post-war economic architecture, the ITO negotiations proved particularly difficult. Although 'approximately ninety per cent of the text of the charter' (ITO Report, 1947: 361) had been agreed ahead of the 1947 Havana Conference on Trade and Employment (which was designed to finalize and agree the ITO), the outstanding 10 per cent covered areas particularly important to the United States (such as on rules governing balance of payments crises and imperial preference systems). Such were the disagreements over the content of the Charter that economic advisor to the US State Department Herbert Feis chose to comment (1948: 51) that '[a]lmost every one . . . [was] trying to re-write important sections of the [Charter], in the service of its special necessities, ideas, wishes or prejudices'. Feis suggested that the number of amendments 'runs into hundreds'. Clair Wilcox (1949a: 47–9) put the figure at 800 and suggested that 'among them as many as two hundred . . . would have destroyed the very foundations of the enterprise'. The US response was to look for a more effective means of securing trade gains; and it did so in the form of a much more focused, lither 'mini-lateral' agreement (the GATT).

The GATT was initially intended to be a stop-gap measure designed to kick-start post-war trade liberalization as well as a means of accelerating the conclusion of the ITO negotiations in much the same way the TPP and TTIP agreements are part of an attempt to force the pace and agenda of the DDA. The round of negotiations out of which it was created (the first round, 1947) resulted from strong pressure from a US delegation anxious to make the most of the president's authority to negotiate tariff reductions prior to its expiry (Finlayson and Zacher, 1981: 562). The outcome was an agreement among a small group of contracting parties to begin the process of liberalizing trade in manufactures, semi-manufactured and capital goods, but not agriculture. And although the round was 'successful' in that it set post-war liberalization in motion, it was not without tension and almost collapsed[2] over a dispute between the USA and UK over the latter's imperial preference system (Kock, 1969: 70).

Disagreements notwithstanding, the Havana conference was eventually concluded and 53 states signed the Final Act of the

United Nations Conference on Trade and Employment (UNCTE) comprising the ITO Charter. The conclusion of the conference was, however, the high point for the ITO. Of the 53 signatory states, only two sought its ratification – Australia and Liberia (ITO Report, 1950: 325). In December 1950 President Truman announced the decision to postpone indefinitely plans for US participation in the ITO stating that the Havana Charter would not be resubmitted to Congress for approval (*New York Herald Tribune*, 7 December 1950). This was followed in February 1951 with similar announcements from the UK and the Netherlands (ITO Report, 1951: 384–5). It was, in the end, an organization that did not serve US interests. The GATT, however, did.

It was not just the commercial focus of the GATT that was designed to reflect the interests of its lead architect (which, because of the need for US goods in war-ravaged economies, also served the short-term interests of others, particularly the European states); the legal framework of the *General Agreement* itself was crafted in such a way that it was congruous with US needs. The GATT was crafted around existing US commercial methods, legal frameworks, styles of negotiating and economic ideas; and the *General Agreement's* extension to new contracting parties over time embedded these methods, frameworks, styles and ideas as the *modus operandi* for liberalization. As Feis put it:

> the American government was eager to preserve in as much of the world as possible the American type of trading system; one shaped mainly to private initiative and calculation, ruled mainly by competition, nominally open to all on equal terms, unclamped by rigid controls. (Feis, 1948: 41)

The result was the construction of a commercial framework that drew from, and entrenched, practices and principles long used within the United States (see Winham, 2006 for an innovative discussion) as well as in relations with its primary trading partners. This was manifest in, among other things, the use of the principles of most-favoured-nation (MFN), national treatment and reciprocity as cornerstones of post-war commercial regulation (principles that are examined in more detail in the next chapter).

What the creation of the GATT did, then, was install a mechanism for liberalizing trade that:

(i)   was multilateral in form;
(ii) reflected the economic needs and commercial practices of its dominant architect;
(iii) offered co-opted partner states the prospect of reconstruction through the entry of US goods into domestic markets at cheaper rates in return for a financial assistance package and the promise of development through reciprocal tariff cuts in US markets; and
(iv) facilitated the liberalization of those sectors at the cutting edge of US industrialization (largely manufactures, semi-manufactures and capital goods) while forestalling liberalization in areas of political and economic sensitivity (at that point in time largely agriculture).

This machinery, in turn, entrenched a set of opportunity structures – by which I mean areas of economic potential – that would contribute to the expansion of the US economy and assist in the preservation of its pre-eminence while at the same time offering fellow signatories the prospect of trade-led reconstruction.

The GATT in operation

For all of the effort expended in crafting a system of trade governance none of the early rounds produced spectacular results (they were certainly not as forthcoming as some of the literature on the early years of the GATT suggests – see, for instance, Gilpin, 2001: 6). Yet, the point is not that each of the early rounds saw less-than-spectacular liberalization, it is rather that the achievements of these first rounds lie elsewhere. While the relatively lacklustre liberalization gains proved frustrating for the delegations involved, the real value of the first rounds lay in:

(i)   consolidating the GATT's role as the centre point for global trade governance and liberalization;
(ii) socializing contracting parties into a particular style of operating wherein negotiations were structured around the (largely bilateral) deals brokered between the most significant trading nations;
(iii) contributing to the post-war rehabilitation of the world economy; and
(iv) helping cement a post-war US-centred sphere of influence which was as strategic as it was economic.

What occurred in the years that followed was the consolidation of the narrow and selective fashion in which the GATT was deployed. Several features of the GATT system are noteworthy in this regard. First, slower-than-expected European reconstruction in the immediate post-war years reinforced an almost exclusive concentration on the liberalization of industrial, manufactured and some semi-manufactured goods as drivers of post-war recovery. Second, despite persistent pressure from Australia and other key contracting parties, the unwillingness of the United States and its European Allies to open up agriculture to negotiation resulted in its *de facto* exclusion from the GATT's remit. Third, in response to acute competition from East, South and South East Asia, measures were put in place to formally exclude textiles and clothing from the liberalization process. In the first instance, this consisted of extracting a series of voluntary quotas limiting imports from Japan, Hong Kong, Pakistan and India offering European and North American producers competitive respite. Thereafter these restrictions were codified first during the Dillon Round (1960–1) with the negotiation of the *Short-Term Agreement on Cotton Textiles*. This, in turn, morphed into the 1962 *Long-Term*

Agreement Regarding Trade in Cotton Textiles and subsequently the 1974 *Multi-Fibre Arrangement* (MFA) (see Heron and Richardson, 2008; and Heron, 2012 for more extensive treatments).

Fourth, although the ranks of the GATT were swollen by the rush of new signatories that sought to accede to the *General Agreement* in the post-war years, a large proportion were not involved in successive trade rounds or bound by their outcome. Indeed, once the second round had been completed in 1949 – a point in time that pre-dates most of the subsequent accession to the GATT – it was not until the Uruguay round (1986–94) that all of the contracting parties agreed to be bound by the results of the negotiations.[3] Even then not all the contracting parties that agreed to be bound by the results were actively engaged in the discussions. Successive rounds, nevertheless, saw the United States and the other leading industrial countries exchange concessions further stimulating trade in manufactured, semi-manufactured and industrial goods. Those countries that chose not to, or were unable to, participate in the negotiations did not benefit from the concession-exchanging activities of their industrial counterparts. The result was to widen the gap between the opportunities afforded to the industrial states and their developing counterparts while at the same time excluding the latter from any say in the negotiations themselves (and as a consequence in the institution's on-going development).

Fifth, the selective and instrumental nature of the GATT was further enhanced by the way the negotiations were organized. The gulf in the opportunities afforded to the industrial and developing countries alike was widened further by the product-by-product, principal supplier method of conducting tariff negotiations wherein a country could only be requested to make tariff cuts on a particular product by the principal supplier of that product to that country (see Wilkinson and Scott, 2008: 486–8). The problem was that developing countries were seldom principal suppliers of anything and were certainly not significant players in world trade in more than one or a handful of products. Their exports were mostly concentrated in raw materials, which generally entered the industrialized countries duty-free anyway (Kock, 1969: 232). Their lack of principal-supplier status precluded them from sitting at the main negotiating table. And their lack of significance across a range of products ensured that they had little say in the negotiations as a whole.

It was only during the fourth round (1956) that GATT rules were altered to allow countries to act collectively in requesting concessions – that is, as collective principal suppliers (GATT, 1956: 80; Kock, 1969: 101). Even then, however, developing countries were at a disadvantage (logistically as well as capacity-wise) in that they had to co-ordinate action among a potentially large number of highly diverse countries in order to meet the requirements of collective principal supplier status. Furthermore, developing countries were effectively prevented from requesting concessions on items that they did not produce in large quantities but in which they hoped to expand production. The effect was that rather than resulting in reductions in barriers to trade that would have been of benefit to all contracting parties, the principal-supplier rule structured the negotiations around the commercial interests of the industrial countries. This, in turn, ensured not only that fewer trade opportunities were realized, it also shut many developing countries out of setting the tone and agenda of the negotiations as well as in having a say in how the institution evolved.

Sixth, the idea behind the use of the principal-supplier rule was that the marginalization of non-principal suppliers would be mitigated by the process of extending tariff concessions on a MFN basis, allowing tariff cuts to trickle down. The problem, however, was that very little of the liberalization agreed among the industrial states proved beneficial to developing countries precisely because the GATT's primary focus was increasing the volume and value of trade among the industrial states in manufactures, semi-manufactures and capital goods and not agriculture, and textiles and clothing (see Brown, 1950; Hudec, 1990: 57). The GATT was not designed to be – nor were claims made that it would become – an instrument for facilitating economic development in the periphery. As a result, developing countries were not only locked out of negotiations by the fact that they were not principal suppliers, their plight was compounded by a perception that this situation would be rectified by gaining concessions through the multilateralization process (that is, the extension of concessions negotiated among two or a small number of parties to all others on a MFN basis).

Seventh, matters were made worse by the expectation that all contracting parties to the GATT should reciprocate for concessions received. For those developing countries that participated in the negotiations this proved troublesome. Not only were they excluded from negotiating meaningful opportunities by dint of not being principal suppliers, and as a result being frozen out of having a say in the form and content of the negotiations, they were required to reciprocate for the concessions they received through the multilateralization process – concessions that, as we have seen, were of dubious value anyway. As Indian Ambassador K. B. Lall commented at the time:

> The developing countries of course had no bargaining power, politically or economically. The rule of reciprocity has required them to give a matching concession, but clearly they were not in a position to give any. While over the last fifteen years, tariffs on industrial products of interest to industrial nations have been gradually brought down, those on products of interest to developing countries have remained at a high level. (Lall, 1965: 174–9)

While this problem was widely recognized it was not until the introduction of Part IV of the GATT (agreed in 1965, effective in 1966) that remedial measures began to be put in place. Yet, the solution that was adopted – removing the requirement to reciprocate – inadvertently made matters worse. By removing the requirement to reciprocate, developing countries were further locked out of the negotiations as they were perceived to have nothing to contribute and their participation was deemed to be even more peripheral (see Srinivasan, 1998: 24).

Eighth, the GATT's almost exclusive focus on tariffs as the only trade restriction discussed during negotiations consolidated further the imbalance in opportunities. For those developing countries exporting tropical products, the primary impediments to their exports were often internal taxes in importing – that is, in industrial country – markets rather than tariffs. Internal taxes, however, were not on the agenda for discussion and requests could not be made for their reduction. Many exports from developing countries were also restricted in the post-war years by quotas put in place ostensibly to protect against adverse balance of payments situations but which were not a part of the negotiations. As each country's balance of payments improved these restrictions were supposed to be lifted. However, as the industrialized countries undertook this process they tended not to lift quotas on products exported by developing countries. As the Committee on Trade and Development noted in 1961 'less-developed countries, as a group, have not benefited significantly from the widely observed movement towards trade liberalization by industrialized countries as a result of their emergence from balance of payments difficulties' (GATT, 1962: 187).

As the GATT evolved and its ranks were swollen by new signatories, pressure grew for it to be altered to take more account of the needs of developing countries. In the main, the response of the Contracting Parties (as the committee-of-the-whole) was to offer developing countries concessions that had little or (more often than not) no impact on the distribution of economic opportunity generated by the GATT. Many of the concessions took the form of declarations and statements of intent – such as the 1961 declaration on the Promotion of the Trade of Less-Developed

Countries – or else comprised limited concessions that had little impact – such as the adoption of Part IV (see Evans, 1971: 121; Srinivasan, 1998: 24). While these concessions raised the prospect that developing countries would reap some benefit, and secured their continued participation, the lack of compunction and the reliance on the goodwill of industrial states ensured that more often than not little was forthcoming. Indeed, it was only with the agreement of the so-called 'Enabling Clause' as part of the 1979 Tokyo accords that real preferential treatment was accorded to developing and least-developed countries, albeit coming with the expectation that developing countries reciprocate appropriately in future trade negotiations (see Yusuf, 1980).

Consolidating matters

By the mid 1960s the character of the GATT as a selective and strategic liberalization device but nonetheless a centre-point for global commercial regulation had been clearly established. The peculiar circumstances of the GATT's birth had, however, ensured that up until this point the development of the institution had been largely informal. Few hard-and-fast rules had been adopted and the contracting parties (more properly, its principal architects) had demonstrated a distinct aversion to formal institutionalization and bureaucratization – as Gilbert Winham (2006: 2) put it, 'mostly the regime developed through customary practice'. This had initially been seen as a strength as the absence of an extensive set of highly prescriptive rules lent it a streamlined, informal and, crucially, malleable quality (Gorter, 1954: 7–8). Unlike the ITO, it was perceived to be neither a tightly binding set of rules nor a constraint on sovereign autonomy (a feature that was particularly important to the United States). While this fluid character initially served the political and economic interests of the GATT's most economically significant contracting parties, and was far from beneficial to its smaller, more vulnerable, developing, primary and agricultural-producing counterparts in that formal and informal rules governing behaviour were often changed on the hop, it did so only in the early years. Thereafter, pressure was increasingly brought to bear for a formalization of GATT disciplines that locked in existing ways of operating.

The Tokyo round (1973–9) ushered in a codification of international trade rules. With this codification came an extension, consolidation and amplification of the inequalities of opportunity that arose from the way GATT rules were deployed. While the results of the round may have produced a more visible and extensive system of international trade law, instead of attenuating existing asymmetries the shift away from 'broad statements of principle' to 'detailed legalisms' simply made them worse (Ostry, 1997: 89). Moreover, the Tokyo round failed to address many of the GATT's defects. Though progress was made on non-tariff barriers, the round resulted in the negotiation of a clutch of side agreements (comprising, among others, the so-called Tokyo 'codes', the forerunners to the WTO's plurilateral agreements) that were binding for (and, as a result, beneficial to) only a handful of (largely) industrial signatories. Little movement was made in liberalizing agricultural markets. The United States continued to dish out lavish export subsidies to domestic producers and impose quotas on imports of dairy produce; and European discrimination in the sector was exacerbated by the further development of its Common Agricultural Policy (CAP). Similarly, the round oversaw the continued exclusion of textiles and clothing from the GATT's remit first with the negotiation of the MFA and then with the extension of discrimination under MFA II. The result was the fabrication of yet another layer of regulation that built upon and entrenched existing asymmetry and inequity.

It was not until the Uruguay round (1986–94) that a concerted effort to broaden the GATT's commercial remit to include those areas of economic interest to developing countries took place. Yet, rather than attending to the asymmetries of opportunity that previous rounds of the GATT had produced, the Uruguay round actually presided over their perpetuation and amplification. It was, as Ostry put it, 'a bum deal' (Ostry, 2007: 28) in which the 'rich countries cut their tariffs by less in the Uruguay Round than poor ones' (*Economist*, 1999). As Nelson Mandela (1998) put it in his speech to the 1998 Geneva ministerial conference celebrating the 50th anniversary of the multilateral trading system:

> We must be frank in our assessment of the outcome of the Uruguay Round. The developing countries were not able to ensure that the rules accommodated their realities. For understandable reasons it was mainly the preoccupations and problems of the advanced industrial economies that shaped the agreement. The sections dealing with the developing countries and the least-developed countries were not adequately thought through.

The conclusion of the Uruguay round saw the inclusion of agreements on agriculture, and textiles and clothing within a wider suite of trade agreements administered by the soon-to-be-created WTO and the adoption of a range of provisions throughout the organization's legal framework designed to ease some of the pressure for reform generated by the new rules. It also resulted in the adoption of agreements on services (the General Agreement on Trade in Services – GATS), intellectual property (the Agreement on Trade Related Intellectual Property Rights – TRIPs) and investment measures (the Agreement on Trade Related Investment Measures – TRIMs).

Yet, while the inclusion of agriculture, and textiles and clothing rectified an existing imbalance in the way the GATT had previously been deployed and the sprinkling of development-sensitive provisions represented a step forward from the GATT era, the introduction of new rules in services, intellectual property and investment measures simply generated additional asymmetry. While under Uruguay rules developing states could finally hope to benefit from the liberalization of agricultural and textiles and clothing markets, their lack of capacity and resources ensured that this was not to be the case in the new areas. The potential fruits of Uruguay were, however, much tastier for the industrial states. Not only were they existing beneficiaries of trade liberalization in areas covered by GATT rules, their economic make-up ensured they would be the principal beneficiaries of the market opportunities presented by the liberalization of services and investment measures, and the codification of trade-related intellectual property rights.

What Uruguay clearly did, then, was to further divide up the arenas of economic activity in which member states could specialize and, in so doing, accentuated the problems facing developing countries seeking to diversify their export portfolios. Moreover, not only were the industrial states better suited to taking advantage of these new rules, their ability to utilize the market opportunities presented therein enabled them to develop a competitive advantage over future market entrants. The result was to carry across the transition from GATT to WTO an asymmetry of economic opportunity that forms the basis upon which the Doha round has ensued and which underpins the tensions that exist among members.

Beyond Uruguay

Unsurprisingly, the Uruguay agreements proved to be a source of frustration from the outset; and efforts to extend the trade agenda further in the wake of the round were greeted with hostility from many developing countries. At the core of developing-country concerns was the growing problem of implementation. It quickly became apparent that not only were a number of developing countries struggling with the requirements of the Uruguay round agreements, there was a good deal of foot-dragging and back-sliding on the part of their industrial counterparts. Tensions were exacerbated by suggestions that the WTO's remit be extended to include investment, government procurement, competition policy, trade facilitation, environmental protection and, most controversially, labour standards (the so-called Singapore issues

– Haworth, Hughes and Wilkinson, 2005: 1944–7),[4] and that the members embark on a further round of trade negotiations so soon after the conclusion of the round.

This tension played out over successive WTO ministerial conferences, each building on the last in terms of the degree of consternation involved. Most infamously, tensions came to a head during the November/December 1999 Seattle ministerial conference when, amid mass demonstrations outside the convention centre delegates failed to agree the launch of what was then touted as the 'millennium round'. They were also notable features of the Cancún (2003) and Hong Kong (2005) conferences and caustic undercurrents of the subsequent and far less dramatic Geneva (2009, 2011) and Bali events (see Scott and Wilkinson, 2010; 2013b; Wilkinson, Hannah and Scott, 2014).

Crucially the post-Seattle rehabilitation process saw a concerted effort to place development at the centre of a new trade round. This, combined with the effort put into building a consensus by key WTO officials (including the then DG Mike Moore) and the tenderness of the political climate in which the Doha ministerial meeting took place (just two months after the 11 September 2001 attacks in the United States), proved enough for members to agree to a new round – albeit named the 'Doha Development Agenda' (DDA) in an attempt to highlight its intended focus. Yet despite its moniker, the DDA promised merely to address a handful of existing anomalies in return for a further extension of the WTO's legal framework into new areas.

There were undoubted successes in tailoring the work programme towards areas of interest to the developing world: the Ministerial Declaration was steeped in the language of development; the Ministerial Decision on Implementation-Related Issues and Concerns (WTO, 2001b) and the Ministerial Declaration identified implementation issues as an integral part of the work programme – albeit the former lacked real compunction; the agricultural negotiations set out to pursue substantial

improvements in market access, reduce (and eventually elimi-
nate) export subsidies and trade-distorting domestic support
systems; the negotiations on non-agricultural market access were
structured such that the reduction and elimination of tariff peaks,
high tariffs, tariff escalation, tariffs affecting the export interests
of developing countries and non-tariff barriers sat alongside a
more traditional focus on the reduction of barriers to trade; the
TRIPs negotiations included a commitment to extend the protection of geographical indicators to products other than wines
and spirits; the Declaration on TRIPs and public health offered
members greater flexibility in adhering to the TRIPs agreement in times of national health crises (WTO, 2001c; Sell, 2014:
73–4); and the Ministerial Declaration promised to explore the
relationship between trade, debt and finance, the plight of small
economies, the transfer of technology, technical co-operation and
capacity building, and a commitment to review and strengthen
special and differential provisions.

However, the balance of potential gains from the work programme remained firmly with the industrial states. In addition
to the benefits resulting from the full implementation of the
Uruguay accords, improvements in non-agricultural market
access (NAMA), aspects of the negotiations on agriculture, and a
further extension of the TRIPs, the DDA added a commitment to
begin (albeit on the basis that an 'explicit consensus' should be
forthcoming) negotiations in investment, government procurement, trade facilitation and competition policy (and possibly a fifth
area, e-commerce) (WTO, 2001a). Moreover, the DDA put in place
a specific time frame in which negotiations would commence on
the Singapore issues (subject to minor clarification, after the mid-
term review of negotiations in Cancún) and stipulated that the
results would form the basis of a second single undertaking.

Unsurprisingly, the imbalances in the DDA were quickly realized and became the source of developing-country frustrations.
The result was a bout of alliance warfare that saw coalition upon

coalition combine and consolidate to produce a deadlock. This, in turn, contributed to the collapse of the 2003 Cancún ministerial conference (see Narlikar and Wilkinson, 2004). Indeed, the only common ground that emerged was that the DDA would not reach a conclusion before its scheduled 1 January 2005 deadline.

After an initial period of reflection, and much like Seattle, the post-Cancún period saw renewed energy emerge among the WTO membership. Breaking the ice, in early 2004 both the United States and European Union signalled that they were ready to negotiate the elimination of all forms of agricultural export subsidies (including credits and food aid – US tools to promote exports – as well as more traditional means of subsidizing exports) (Clapp, 2004: 1444). By June 2004 then-WTO DG Supachai Panitchpakdi was praising delegates for the progress that had been made in the agricultural negotiations (albeit peppered with the obligatory encouragement to keep moving forward). Each of the principal protagonists in the Cancún showdown had submitted papers outlining their preferred ways of moving forward – the Group of 20, Group of 10 and Group of 33 – and the European Union again stressed its willingness to phase out export subsidies on the condition that other (largely US) forms of subsidizing exports were eliminated and that an 'acceptable' outcome could be reached on market access and domestic support (WTO, 2004). These developments nevertheless proved insufficient to enable members to agree upon formal negotiating modalities at the 2005 Hong Kong ministerial. The result was a decision to scale back expectations ahead of the conference to ensure that some agreement was reached and to lock in the momentum that had been built in the negotiations since the collapse at Cancún (Wilkinson, 2006c).

The conclusion of the Hong Kong ministerial proved to be a high point. The April 2006 deadline for the agreement of negotiating modalities agreed in Hong Kong was missed; little progress was made in the negotiations generally; and the round came to an abrupt halt in July 2006. Repeated attempts thereafter failed to inject new momentum into the round and the negotiations formally collapsed in July 2008 (see Ismail, 2009b: 579–605; also Ismail, 2012). It was not until the run-up to the 2013 Bali ministerial conference that negotiating began again in earnest, albeit members proved unable to agree a deal ahead of the meeting. The result – despite intentions of successive DGs otherwise – was that the Bali conference saw a return to ministerial conferences as negotiation sessions. What ensured was a frenetic bout of negotiating over five long days wherein hopes were raised, dashed, raised and almost dashed again before members agreed to a small package of measures covering three broad areas (trade facilitation, agriculture, and special and differential treatment for least-developed countries – see Wilkinson, Hannah and Scott, 2014 for a fulsome account).

The agreement reached in Bali was notable because it marked the first multilateral agreement reached in the WTO since the organization began operations on 1 January 1995. It was not, however, a game-changing moment marking a new era in the multilateral trading system correcting past imbalances or inequities, or closing the gap between developed and developing countries alike. Rather, Bali continued the pattern of asymmetrical bargains by agreeing a deal that would bring greater benefits to the industrial countries (via the Agreement on Trade Facilitation) in exchange for limited concessions in agriculture (relating to public stockpiling of foodstuffs) and a small package of measures designed to help LDCs. In the *longue durée* of the multilateral trading system, Bali was very much business as usual underlining – rather than ameliorating – the case for root-and-branch reform of the multilateral trading system.

Conclusion

What we see, then, the development of a form of global trade governance in which the distribution of economic opportunity

among GATT/WTO members has become increasingly asymmetrical. The manner in which the GATT was first deployed
saw the selective liberalization of markets in areas of economic
interest to the *General Agreement*'s founder contracting parties.
This was consolidated and amplified by the subsequent exclusion of agriculture, and textiles and clothing from the GATT's
purview and the concentration on the liberalization of industrial, manufactured and some semi-manufactured goods. This
pattern of asymmetry was further exacerbated and entrenched
by the conclusion of the Tokyo negotiations; it was institutionalized, consolidated and extended by the bargain struck during the
Uruguay round; and it has been amplified further by the bargain
struck in Bali. The result has been to provide industrial states
with market opportunities in core and leading-edge sectors while
enabling them to protect and/or forestall liberalization in others;
whereas, developing countries have been bought off with a range
of limited concessions and market opportunities that bring with
them the promise of trade-led growth. In this way, the GATT/
WTO has amply fulfilled its role as a key strategic device.

This institutional history matters not only because it explains
why we have the system that we do, it also enables us to see
precisely why this pattern of asymmetrical bargaining looks set
to continue. Current progress in the Doha round suggests that
many developing states will be able to do little more than consolidate their production of agricultural produce, textiles and
clothing, and some low technology goods. Yet, they will do so
– as least with regard to agriculture – without the benefit of significant market access improvements into industrial countries.
Little industrial diversification will occur among the poorest or
smallest economies as the costs of moving away from established industries and investing in new sectors will be prohibitive
albeit significant opportunities may lie therein (see Hoekman,
2011; and Hoekman and Mattoo, 2007). This is irrespective of
any increase in technical and other assistance that aid for trade

packages may provide. The leading industrial states will nevertheless be able to consolidate their competitive and comparative advantages in sectors in which they are already dominant, thereby further crowding out the capacity of developing countries to be market entrants (and reinforcing their concentration in first-phase industrial production). Such an outcome will see the DDA result in significantly less than the development round it was supposed to be. Yet, by the time the round actually concludes such will be the elation that a conclusion has been reached many will barely notice that another unequal bargain has been struck – to which the celebrations that followed the conclusion of the Bali ministerial bear testimony.

That said, understanding the way the current system of trade governance has evolved is only part of the story. All that we have observed so far is why the system has evolved in the manner that it has and the form of governance that it has produced. We have yet to explore the mechanisms driving the evolution of this system, the means by which asymmetrical bargains are produced, or why – unless fundamental change takes place – this form of institutional evolution is likely to continue. To do this we need to explore precisely how a pattern of enduring (and growing) asymmetry has come to be a feature of the regime we actually have. It is to this task that the next chapter turns.

CHAPTER TWO

Bargaining among unequals

If the first part of our effort to rethink how we govern global trade is to understand the more strategic and instrumental character of the GATT/WTO explored in Chapter 1, the second part is to better appreciate how asymmetrical outcomes have been, and are produced – the task of this chapter. To do this we need to get to the very heart of how the system works. We need to understand its internal machinery and to explore the mechanisms by which trade is governed and outcomes generated. Only then can we understand precisely what needs to be done to correct what is wrong with the WTO.

Like many intergovernmental organizations the GATT/WTO draws from a set of principles to justify its existence and which establish its *raison d'être*. The World Health Organization, for example, draws from principles designed to realize 'the happiness, harmonious relations and security of all peoples' (WHO, 1946: para. 1). Similarly, the International Labour Organization's (ILO) Declaration of Philadelphia specifies that,

> labour is not a commodity; freedom of expression and of association are essential to sustained progress; poverty anywhere constitutes a danger to prosperity everywhere; and the war against want requires . . . unrelenting vigour within each nation, and . . . continuous and concerted international effort. (ILO, 1944)

In contrast, the GATT/WTO's core principles are much more prescriptive than merely guiding behaviour or lending character to a system; that is, they are not mere desiderata, specifying what the functioning of the organization aims to achieve. Rather, they are the very mechanics of global trade governance. They structure relations between and among member states shaping what can and cannot be done, allowing some states greater agency than others in operationalizing as well as in taking advantage of the rules. In so doing, the GATT/WTO's principles underpin the production of substantive outcomes that have a real-world impact – as we have seen generating trade openings in some areas providing a stimulus for industrial expansion or new development, and producing and maintaining trade closings in other areas negatively affecting employment opportunities and so on.

Identifying the *constitutive* principle that lends the WTO its character is, however, a little harder than at first appears to be the case. In the case of the ILO, the pursuit of social justice defines the organization – that is, it constitutes what it seeks to do and how it seeks to do it. Most of the literature – and indeed the WTO itself[5] – points to MFN, reciprocity and national treatment as the foundational principles of the multilateral trading system. These principles are expressed in the preamble to the GATT in the requirement that contracting parties enter 'into reciprocal and mutually advantageous arrangements directed to the substantial reduction of tariffs and other barriers to trade and to the elimination of discriminatory treatment in international commerce' (GATT, 1986: preamble, para. 2) as they are in the substantive articles of the *General Agreement* itself (most significantly articles I, III, XVII, XXVIII, XXVIII*bis*, XXXVI, *ad*XXXVI) as well as in the *Agreement Establishing the World Trade Organization* (para. 1). They are framed within, as well as justified in terms of a recognition that 'relations in the field of trade and economic endeavour should be conducted with a view to raising standards of living, ensuring full employment and a large and steadily growing volume of real income and effective demand, developing the full use of the resources of the world and expanding the production and exchange of goods' (GATT, 1986: preamble, para. 1) 'while allowing for the optimal use of the world's resources in accordance with the objective of sustainable development' (WTO, 1994: para. 1).

Yet, MFN, national treatment and reciprocity are not actually the constitutive principles we might at first suppose; that is, they do not define the system, give it its character, or determine its functioning. Rather, they are second-order, operational principles that manage (but not determine) aspects of trade negotiations. MFN requires – certain exceptions aside[6] – that each member treats all other members as if they were their most favoured trading partners; national treatment requires that foreign and domestically produced goods and services are treated in the same way (taxation and regulation-wise) once they have entered a market; and reciprocity behoves member states to offer their trading partners concessions of roughly equivalent value to those received during negotiations.[7]

The global trade regime's first order – that is, its constitutive – principle is much more adversarial than MFN, national treatment and reciprocity, and determines how each of these second-order principles is operationalized. The primary and constitutive principle is *competition*. The global trade regime is a system of order generated by the outcomes of competitive negotiations. Member states are pitched against one another in strategic games wherein bargains are negotiated through the deployment of various means (strategic, material and otherwise) in settings that shape their interaction. The bargains that these interactions produce generate trade opportunities, rules governing the conduct of negotiations, procedures for the administration of the system, and precedents that affect all aspects of the system's operation.

Thus, competition lends the system its character, and the adversarial nature of negotiations – as well as the crises that periodically afflict each round – are the defining features of global trade governance. Certainly there are other aspects of the system that appear not to be based on competition – dispute settlement, trade policy review, and, more recently, data and knowledge gathering. Yet, each of these attributes is itself a second-order appendage that has developed from the functioning of this competitive and adversarial system. Dispute settlement arose out of a need to mediate between parties failing to adhere to the outcome of negotiations (a facility which, though enhanced in the move from GATT to WTO, has not particularly assisted the capacity of developing countries to redress imbalances in the dispute settlement process – see Busch and Reinhardt, 2003; also Zeng, 2013); trade policy review emerged as a surveillance mechanism for ensuring that members made good on the commitments they promised and to render visible the more mysterious aspects of their political economies; and recent moves to become a serious source of trade data and knowledge – functions that were always part of what the secretariat did but which were previously done only as much as was necessary – about the multilateral trading system have developed to lend credibility to an institution (particularly a secretariat) that has felt increasingly embattled as the Doha round has stuttered to a halt.

To announce that competition is the foundational and constitutive principle of the system appears, at one level, to be rather obvious. This is far from the case, however. Understanding that this is a system that generates outcomes and systems of rules that result from contestations between and among members varying dramatically in size, economic significance and negotiating capacity immediately calls into question suggestions that fair and equitable bargains can, or could ever be produced. In any form of adversarial contest, outcomes reflect distributions of power. While these distributions may comprise aspects that are benevolent and 'good' or trade-offs that result in concessions given for acquiescence they nonetheless reflect and speak primarily to the interests of the most powerful. Yet, nowhere is this made explicit in mainstream accounts of the GATT, the WTO or the multilateral trading system. Instead, as Singer puts it, 'we tend to think of trade as something politically neutral' (2004: 96) and, we might add, to assume that by some mysterious process the outcomes that result will not be the consequence – or a reflection – of power politics. We need to disavow ourselves of this view.

Of course fleeting and off-the-cuff references to the adversarial nature of trade politics do appear in the literature, albeit they seldom form the starting point of an analysis and are often presented in a more general context in which the system is constructed in predominantly neutral and power-political ways. In these more fleeting references, this system is variously described as 'war by other means' or akin to a game of chess (Grossman and Helpman, 1995; McKenna, 2013), though neither metaphor has more than superficial value. The rules of war and of chess are more complex and perhaps refined than those governing trade negotiations. Both the capacity of members to compete as adversaries and the parameters in which that competition takes place shapes outcomes; and it is these outcomes that govern how trade takes place. MFN, national treatment and reciprocity certainly have a bearing on the negotiations – with the first two shaping the calculations of what each member deems to be of roughly equivalent value – but it is competition that determines the character of the system and which determines how these second-order principles are applied. And competition is a principle that when applied among adversaries differing dramatically in size, capacity and understanding in a context wherein the rules favour the strong over the weak is hardly commensurate with either the production of equitable outcomes or a fair and legitimate system of governance.

The aims of this chapter are to show how the WTO's adversarial system operates, to illustrate how that system shapes negotiating outcomes, and to demonstrate why the organization of trade in this way is likely to lead us further away from, rather than closer to, a more equitable trade order. In building on the argument of the preceding chapter – that our persistence with a system that has only limited value to its members as a whole and which exacerbates the inequitable distribution of economic opportunities among them is unsustainable – my argument here is that an adversarial system of trade governance cannot hope to promote equitable trade-led growth for all and any reformed system must in the long term be built on less competitive foundations.

In developing its argument, the chapter unfolds in three parts. The first part explores the differentials in capabilities that exist across member states: that is, how giants negotiate with Lilliputians. Here, the chapter explores not only the relative significance of each country in global trade, it also explores the differences that exist in the capacity of states to engage in negotiations in the first place (inasmuch as the size of missions and technical capacity to which they point tell us anything). The second part focuses on the institutional context in which adversarial competition takes place, the outcome of which is the principal means by which global trade is governed. Here I focus on the rules and norms as well as the wider strategic environments that shape the context in which trade negotiations take place. The third section focuses on the forms of behaviour that this system of governance gives rise to, accounting for why trade politics is so contested and why this contestation ensures that in the long run the system is unsustainable.

Of giants and Lilliputians

If trade were governed by the outcomes of negotiations that took place among 160 members differing dramatically in size, capability, importance in world trade, in the *absence* of a system of rules developed to open some sectors while preserving protection in others in ways that spoke to the economic interests of the system's dominant states, we would still expect these adversarial contests to produce asymmetrical outcomes. Indeed, bargains between states have been and are always affected by the relative distribution of capabilities. While examples do exist of contests producing unexpected outcomes, when smaller and less powerful states are able to leverage favourable outcomes from bigger more powerful states, these are the exception rather than the rule. Larger, able, more powerful states tend to triumph over their smaller, less able and less powerful counterparts. This is as true in trade as it is in war (research on asymmetrical warfare notwithstanding – Mack, 1975; Arreguín-Toft, 2001) and other forms of international negotiation (Huntington, 1993; Zartman and Rubin, 2002). As Thomas Pogge puts it, the 'design of this order [the WTO]' is one in which the leading industrial states 'enjoy a crushing advantage in bargaining power and expertise' (2008: 26–7). So, just how unequally matched are members relative to one another when they face each other as adversaries in trade negotiations?

WTO members are not strictly classified according to established or institutionally specific criteria. What occurs instead is a process of self-declaration in which members declare whether they are developed or developing countries. These declarations normally cohere with those development stratifications used in the UN system – for instance, least-developed countries are identified and treated in accordance with standard UN determinations. Members can and do challenge the self-declarations of others, particularly because there are advantages that may be seen to be accruing to a member that misleadingly self-announces as a developing country (China is perhaps the most significant example of a country whose self-declared status as a developing country has been challenged – see *People's Daily*, 2010); but broadly speaking, the members of each group are widely known.

Of the WTO's 160 members, 21 are – according to IMF classifications (2013: 121) – 'advanced economies'. The remainder – what the Fund refers to as 'emerging market and developing economies' – comprises such a broad array of countries that the monikers 'emerging market' and 'developing economies' appear to make little sense. Yet, labelling them 'emerging markets' and 'developing', while not riding roughshod over the important differences that exist in this group (particularly with regard to those recognized as least developed), suggests they all share a family resemblance that has some value when thinking about how members interact in the WTO and the forms of behaviour that their interaction produces. Certainly, it is the case that the determination of what constitutes an 'advanced economy' is a little arbitrary – the IMF's classification is based on membership of the OECD as it stood in 1990 (minus Turkey). It nevertheless has the effect of dividing members up in ways that suggest (and indeed construct) a commonality of interests and from which flows – whether real or constructed – a sense of identity. Moreover, while there are exceptions to this classification – particularly with regard to the identification of subsets of countries such as the BRICS, New Industrialized Countries (NICs), the Next 11 and so on – it plays an important part in the alliance politics that have come to be a notable feature of the multilateral trading system as well as in the construction of the 'North–South Theatre' (Weiss, 2012a: 50–72). The accusation that one group of countries or another – almost always developing versus developed – is acting unfairly is an all-too-familiar feature of global trade politics, irrespective of whether the real divisions over issues reflects an actual split along developmental lines (however measured). Moreover, the rigid categorization of countries into these two groups has the effect of acting as one component of the wider frame in which member-state interaction takes place, in which the characters of broad sets of countries are already determined and wherein the likelihood of particular forms of behaviour occurring is accentuated.

Yet, despite the dangers of rigidly categorizing states, it is also easy to see why such categories might be useful. What we have seen is that the developed countries have historically been the

Table 2.1. Percentage share of world merchandise (exports and imports) by region (2011)

Exports		Imports	
Region/Country	Percentage	Region/Country	Percentage
World	*100.0*	*World*	*100.0*
Europe	37.1	Europe	38.1
EU	33.9	EU	34.6
Asia	31.1	Asia	30.9
North America	12.8	North America	17.1
Middle East	7.0	Middle East	3.8
South America	4.2	South America	4.0
Africa	3.3	Africa	3.1
WTO members as a whole	*93.8*	*WTO members as a whole*	*95.9*

Source: author's adaptation of WTO, 2012a

disproportionate beneficiaries of the GATT/WTO liberalization. Developing countries have, on the other hand, been the relative losers (or, at the very least, gainers by a lower order of magnitude) with the least developed having received even less. In terms of pursuing a politics of rectification it makes sense to lend weight to arguments for redress by reminding us that the few have been benefiting at the expense of the many. It is equally the case that members do differ dramatically in terms of their relative significance in global trade and their capacity to benefit from any bargains that might be negotiated. The need to be more precise in understanding the economic complexion of members is taken up later in the book. At the moment, suffice it to say that the divisions are as political as they are real.

Tables 2.1–2.5 illustrate the dramatic differences that exist in the economic weight and bargaining capacity of the contestants in WTO negotiations. Table 2.1 sets out the percentage share of regions in world merchandise exports and imports. Table 2.2 ranks the top 50 states in terms of their significance as importers

Table 2.2. Percentage share of top 50 exporters and importers in world merchandise trade (2012)

Rank	Exporter	Share	Rank	Importer	Share
1	China	11.1	1	United States	12.6
2	United States	8.4	2	China	9.8
3	Germany	7.6	3	Germany	6.3
4	Japan	4.3	4	Japan	4.8
5	Netherlands	3.6	5	United Kingdom	3.7
6	France	3.1	6	France	3.6
7	Korea	3.0	7	Netherlands	3.2
8	Russian Federation	2.9	8	Hong Kong	3.0
9	Italy	2.7	9	Korea	2.8
10	Hong Kong	2.7	10	India	2.6
11	United Kingdom	2.6	11	Italy	2.6
12	Canada	2.5	12	Canada	2.6
13	Belgium	2.4	13	Belgium	2.4
14	Singapore	2.2	14	Mexico	2.0
15	Saudi Arabia	2.1	15	Singapore	2.0
16	Mexico	2.0	16	Russian Federation	1.8
17	United Arab Emirates	1.9	17	Spain	1.8
18	Chinese Taipei	1.6	18	Chinese Taipei	1.5
19	India	1.6	19	Australia	1.4
20	Spain	1.6	20	Thailand	1.3
21	Australia	1.4	21	Turkey	1.3
22	Brazil	1.3	22	Brazil	1.3
23	Thailand	1.2	23	United Arab Emirates	1.2
24	Malaysia	1.2	24	Switzerland	1.1

Rank	Country	Value		Rank	Country	Value
25	Switzerland	1.2		25	Malaysia	1.1
26	Indonesia	1.0		26	Poland	1.1
27	Poland	1.0		27	Indonesia	1.0
28	Sweden	0.9		28	Austria	1.0
29	Austria	0.9		29	Sweden	0.9
30	Norway	0.9		30	Saudi Arabia	0.8
31	Czech Republic	0.9		31	Czech Republic	0.8
32	Turkey	0.8		32	South Africa	0.7
33	Qatar	0.7		33	Viet Nam	0.6
34	Kuwait	0.6		34	Hungary	0.5
35	Ireland	0.6		35	Denmark	0.5
36	Nigeria	0.6		36	Norway	0.5
37	Viet Nam	0.6		37	Ukraine	0.5
38	Denmark	0.6		38	Chile	0.4
39	Iran	0.6		39	Slovak Republic	0.4
40	Hungary	0.6		40	Finland	0.4
41	Venezuela	0.5		41	Israel	0.4
42	Iraq	0.5		42	Portugal	0.4
43	Kazakhstan	0.5		43	Romania	0.4
44	South Africa	0.5		44	Egypt	0.4
45	Slovak Republic	0.4		45	Argentina	0.4
46	Argentina	0.4		46	Philippines	0.4
47	Chile	0.4		47	Greece	0.3
48	Angola	0.4		48	Ireland	0.3
49	Finland	0.4		49	Venezuela	0.3
50	Algeria	0.4		50	Colombia	0.3

Source: author's adaptation of WTO, 2013c

Table 2.3. Members with separate dedicated missions to the WTO (as of 26 July 2013)
Australia, Brazil, Canada, Chile, China, Colombia, Costa Rica, Dominican Republic, Ecuador, El Salvador, European Union, Guatemala, Honduras, Hong Kong, Hungary, India, Macao, Malaysia, Mexico, Namibia, New Zealand, Norway, Panama, Pakistan, Philippines, Saudi Arabia, Singapore, Sri Lanka, Switzerland, Taiwan, Thailand, Turkey, United States of America, Uruguay (34)

Source: Geneva Welcome Centre (CAGI) http://www.cagi.ch/en.php (accessed September 2013)

and exporters. In combination we see that North America, Europe (particularly the European Union) and Asia are the largest traders, with South America and Africa being the smallest. Within these regions we see that the United States and China are the most significant trading powers with Japan and the leading European countries not far behind. What we also see is that the difference between the United States, China and the European Union countries, and the rest of the top 50 – let alone the rest of the world – is dramatic.

Representation

Moving beyond the pure trade data, we see a concomitant variation in size and scale of political representation among WTO members. Only 34 have dedicated WTO missions in Geneva (Table 2.3). Sixteen delegations have no representatives based in Geneva at all – though this is an improvement on the 28 members that did not have diplomatic representation prior to the launch of the Doha round in 2001 (Table 2.4) – with many of these members still relying on the representatives based in other European capitals (normally for ACP countries their missions to the EU in Brussels).[8] The remaining 109 have representatives in Geneva that deal with trade issues but which are part of other broader international organization missions. Moreover, of this 109 a significant proportion (but for which precise numbers are not available) of the lesser developed members of this group rep-

| Table 2.4. Non-resident delegations to the WTO (excluding observers) 1999 and 2013 ||
1999	2013
Antigua and Barbuda	Antigua and Barbuda
Belize	Belize
Benin	Dominica
Botswana	Fiji
Burkina Faso	Gambia
Central African Republic	Grenada
Chad	Guyana
Dominica	Malawi
Fiji	Papua New Guinea
Gambia	Saint Kitts and Nevis
Grenada	Saint Lucia
Guinea-Bissau	Saint Vincent and the Grenadines
Guyana	Samoa
Macao	Suriname
Malawi	Tonga
Maldives	Vanuatu
Mali	
Namibia	
Niger	
Papua New Guinea	
Saint Kitts and Nevis	
Saint Lucia	
Saint Vincent and the Grenadines	
Sierra Leone	
Solomon Islands	
Suriname	
Swaziland	
Togo	

Source: WTO 1999a; http://www.wto.org/english/tratop_e/devel_e/genwk_e.htm
(accessed September 213)

resent their country in more than just a WTO capacity – that is, they also have other diplomatic and international organization portfolios.

The data are a little more mixed for the number of personnel each member has representing WTO issues. It is certainly the case that the larger more able trading powers have the largest and most technically able delegations. Moreover, the size of their Geneva-based delegations has increased since the WTO was established despite the well-documented problems in the Doha round. Increases have also been registered in the size of some developing-country representations. A number of factors explain these trends.

First, the realization that the Uruguay negotiations did not bring the gains that the round's conclusion had promised, in conjunction with the launch of a new round (the DDA) during the early stages of which it became clear that the development content was quickly being whittled away, encouraged many developing countries to scale up their representation in Geneva. Second, there has been a growing appreciation of the significance and consequence of international trade rules generally to which many developing countries have responded – an appreciation that has been reinforced over the course of the Doha round (but particularly after the Cancún, 2003, and Hong Kong, 2005, ministerial conferences). Third, some developing countries have become reasonably major exporters and have boosted their representation as a means of leveraging more favourable trade openings. Fourth, a number of developing countries have been able to avail themselves of the growing assistance provided by development-orientated organizations – inter- and non-governmental – in Geneva (such as the South Centre, the International Trade Centre, ITC, the International Centre for Trade and Sustainable Development, ICTSD, to name but three) that has offset some of the costs of establishing dedicated trade missions. Fifth, international assistance programmes have increasingly come to recognize the importance of improving the technical capacity of developing countries which, in turn, have had a positive knock-on effect on representation.

Sixth, some issues are of such significance to the economic fortunes of particular developing countries, and have become so entangled in the wider political contestation of the Doha round, that certain members have enhanced their representation on this basis alone. Benin, Burkina Faso, Chad and Mali,[9] for instance, have moved from a position of having no Geneva representation in 1999 (just before the launch of the DDA – see Table 2.4) to having resident delegations – but not dedicated missions – with staffing levels nominally comparable with major economies (though differences in technical and capital-based capacity remain) precisely because the primary issue of concern to them (cotton) is of acute importance and has become something of a *cause célèbre* in the Doha round (see Lee, 2013). Benin, for instance, has 12 delegates registered (but not necessarily present) in Geneva – the same number as the Russian Federation. Burkina Faso's delegation of 10 is equivalent to that of Australia, France, Spain and Switzerland. Chad has as many Geneva-based delegates as Ireland (7), while Mali's delegation of 6 is a match for Finland, New Zealand and South Africa (see Table 2.5).

These positive developments notwithstanding, it remains the case that the industrial members have a distinct 'Geneva advantage' that, when married to the depth of their nationally based expertise, is considerable (see Table 2.5). What the figures do not illustrate is the extent to which the larger delegations comprise personnel that are more specialized in particular tasks; they say nothing about the size of the domestic-based trade capacity; they do not illustrate the extent to which some countries – particularly members of the European Union – record artificially low numbers of personnel per member country but also have access to a wider EU pool of expertise (for instance, Ireland might only have the same size of delegation as Chad but it also benefits from the

Table 2.5. Number of personnel identified as working on WTO issues for each member state in Geneva

WTO Member	Size of Delegation
China; Japan	22
United States Of America	19
Brazil; Côte d'Ivoire	18
Morocco; Chinese Taipei	17
South Korea	16
European Union	15
Canada	14
Kenya; Mexico; Viet Nam	13
Benin; Cuba; Russian Federation; Thailand	12
Angola; Belgium; Jamaica; Zimbabwe	11
Australia; Botswana; Burkina Faso; Egypt; France; Indonesia; Pakistan; Philippines; Spain; Switzerland; Venezuela	10
Cameroon; Germany; India; Paraguay; Peru; Singapore	9
Argentina; Bangladesh; Gabon; Guatemala; Netherlands; Norway; Qatar; Rwanda; Tanzania; Togo; Turkey; United Kingdom	8
Bahrain; Chad; Chile; Congo; Dominican Republic; Ecuador; Hong Kong; Ireland; Mauritius; Nepal; Trinidad & Tobago; Uganda; Zambia	7
Barbados; Bolivia; Colombia; Finland; Madagascar; Mali; Mauritania; Myanmar; New Zealand; Nigeria; Oman; South Africa; Suriname; Swaziland	6
Antigua & Barbuda; Brunei Darussalam; Croatia; Denmark; Djibouti; El Salvador; Guyana; Haiti; Honduras; Israel; Lithuania; Macao; Malawi; Malaysia; Montenegro; Nicaragua; Papua New Guinea; Saudi Arabia; Ukraine; United Arab Emirates	5
Austria; Burundi; Dominica; Estonia; Gambia; Ghana; Hungary; Iceland; Italy; Jordan; Laos; Lesotho; Maldives; Mozambique; Senegal; Sweden; Uruguay	4
Belize; Cambodia; Central African Republic; Costa Rica; Cyprus; Czech Republic; Greece; Guinea; Kuwait; Liechtenstein; Malta; Niger; Panama; Poland; Portugal; Saint Lucia; Slovak Republic; Tajikistan; FYR Macedonia; Tunisia	3
Albania; Bulgaria; Cape Verde; Congo DRC; Fiji; Georgia; Grenada; Kyrgyz Republic; Latvia; Luxembourg; Moldova; Mongolia; Romania; Saint Kitts & Nevis; Saint Vincent & the Grenadines; Samoa; Sierra Leone; Slovenia; Solomon Islands; Sri Lanka; Tonga; Vanuatu	2
Armenia; Guinea-Bissau; Namibia	1

Source: drawn from WTO Directory, 5 June 2013

existence and size – fifteen – of the EU's delegation); nor do they highlight the very real logistical problems that least-developed and developing countries face. As Debapriya Bhattacharya puts it,

> Let me highlight a specific problem relating to participation, namely, the use of senior officials. For a developed country this means a plane full of lawyers, economists and technical experts from its trade ministry. Recently, the emerging economies have also been following suit in this regard. For the LDCs, the ambassador is the senior official for all practical purposes. He or she is the technical expert and also has to represent ministers, when necessary. The LDCs do not have the capacity to buy air tickets for the experts and keep them in 'expensive' Geneva. Consequently, one sees that there is a big difference between nominal participation and real participation in WTO negotiations. (Bhattacharya, 2008: 3)

One final note is necessary before we move on to talk about the confines in which member negotiations take place. While a greater supply of expertise is now available from which developing countries can draw – both in terms of that provided by the South Centre, ITC and ICTSD among others – it remains the case that the interests of the industrial countries are better served by, and their ideas and interests reflected in a much larger trade community (Lang, 2009; Hannah, 2011; Eagleton-Pierce, 2012; 2013). Inevitably the legal and ideational regimes in which the WTO is embedded and in which members operate have their own biases, the extent of which we have yet to properly appreciate. Nonetheless, what we do know is that they seldom advantage developing countries – particularly the least developed.

Structuring contestation

If differentials in economic significance and technical capacity lend a structure to negotiations in one way – by pitching unequals against one another – then the institutional confines in which their contestation takes place also shapes the nature of their interaction. These institutional confines relate to the rules, norms, procedures, practices and precedents that govern interaction as well as to the physical arrangement of negotiations; and what we know from the literature on institutions generally is that they are not neutral, autonomous entities. We know that their influence on the behaviour and expectations of actors is not marginal, but significant. We know that they structure relations and affect outcomes in a manner that reflects the interests of dominant powers; and we know that institutions themselves are the product of social orders – either as entities helping secure and maintain dominant positions in a particular order (as the GATT was) or else products of oppositional moments and forces (as was the original intention of UNCTAD). In this way, as Kathleen Thelen and Sven Steinmo observe, institutions tend to structure power relations among actors in ways that privilege some while putting others at a disadvantage (Thelen and Steinmo, 1992: 2), and they reflect 'a particular bias, allowing access to some interests while denying it to others and encouraging and highlighting some points of view at the cost of others' (Bulmer and Birch, 1998: 604).

Yet, we also know that institutions develop and change through time. This development and change is the product not only of an institution's interaction with the environment in which it is located, the result of refinements implemented to ensure its smooth functioning, or a direct result of the role for which it was originally created. It is also the result of a degree of institutional autonomy developed through an institution's very functioning. To put it another way, once created institutions develop a life of their own. This is not, however, an existence divorced from the circumstances of an institution's establishment; rather it is a development rooted in an institution's core purposes which itself helps to shape any internal changes as well as, to varying degrees, external circumstances.

That said, we know that much institutional development is incremental. Modifications tend to be at the margins and in keeping with existing formats and ways of operating. They may be a response to a technical problem, such as the need to establish a means of overseeing the administration of a set of rules, or the result of pressure from actors subject to the institution's rules and whose participation is essential to its purposes, but who are not dominant therein. They nevertheless help sustain a developmental trajectory that is knowable and consistent with the purposes for which the institution was created and the interests that it was designed to serve. Hence, institutions not only imbue their architects with certain advantages, they preserve these advantages through time. Moreover, institutional architects tend to put in place significant barriers to new entrants such that challenges to the prevailing configurations of power are attenuated. As Robert Hunter Wade puts it, institutional innovators often seek to 'kick away the ladder' enabling them to perpetuate the advantages accrued to them from the institution's creation (Wade, 2003: 632).

Inevitably, this can ensure that institutions are conflict laden. Indeed, it is precisely because they reflect prevailing configurations of power – that is, they install the powerful in positions of influence and advantage relative to their less-powerful counterparts – that they are also sites of contestation. Thus, to ensure that an institution remains relevant and continues to serve the interests which it was created to serve, institutional development also tends to reflect the outcomes and accommodations resulting from these struggles (see Cox, 1997: 99). It nonetheless remains the case that these accommodations – while offering less-powerful actors concessions to ensure their continued compliance – preserve existing biases as well as implant new ones consistent with prevailing configurations of power.

It is precisely this pattern of behaviour that explains the development of the GATT and its transformation into the WTO. As we saw in the previous chapter, the institution was designed and created to serve a particular set of interests. Its construction imbued the United States and the European powers with what Robert Keohane calls 'first mover advantages' (2002: 253). These first-mover advantages preserved a way of liberalizing trade and put in place significant obstacles to new entrants (the accession process being a good example – see Copelovitch and Ohls, 2012). Moreover, as the last chapter also clearly illustrated, the developments that occurred in the life-cycle of the GATT were largely incremental (the establishment of the WTO was far from transformational as it merely deepened and widened an existing way of managing trade – see Wilkinson, 2005b) and continued to serve the interests of the industrial countries. What we need to do now is establish how the multilateral trading system was able to unfold in this way.

Rules of the game

Surprisingly few rules were determined or have since been negotiated governing the conduct of negotiations. Instead, bargaining has tended to take place on the basis of established norms, customs and practices. Indeed, it was not until well in the GATT's lifecycle that anything approximating rules of engagement governing negotiations were determined. And even when rules were determined they merely put into statute existing ways of operating via what Winham (2006: 2) refers to as 'a modicum of constitutional change'.

As we noted in the previous chapter, in the early years the absence of formal rules and procedures was widely welcomed. Negotiations were largely bilateral and conducted on a product-by-product basis, the results of which were then multilateralized – a style of negotiating that owed more to habit than to thoughtful organization. This not only added to the perception of the GATT as an informal non-sovereignty-threatening agreement (critical to secure the acquiescence of the US Congress as well as other national polities), it also enabled rules to be changed on

the hoof (Wilkinson, 2006a: 46–74). While this suited the leading industrial states, as rules could be altered to ensure that their
interests were best served, the lack of codification beyond broad
and rather vague statements of principle lent little security to
those participants seeking protection against untoward practices.
Moreover, even when GATT rules were codified (and negotiations shifted away from bilateral product-by-product discussions
to the application of a formula) it tended to be done in such a way
that entrenched the very practices that enabled the leading states
to dominate. And it remains the case that other than the broad
statements of principle included in the ministerial declarations
launching a trade round, hard and fast rules governing negotiations are conspicuous by their absence. As Kenneth Dam put it
more than 40 years ago, 'The General Agreement was conceived
as a *product* of . . . negotiations not as a framework for conducting
them' (Dam, 1970: 57, emphasis in original). Little has changed
since.

In place of hard and fast rules, the broad shape of the negotiations was and is given form by three broad principles with the
exact application of these practices determined on the hoof and
subject to change:

(i)   liberalization is achieved through a *political* process of nego-
      tiation among participating states (this is irrespective of the
      application of any formula as the coefficients applied are the
      subject of political debate);
(ii) the bargains struck are designed to produce an *exchange*
      of concessions wherein the currency of exchange is under-
      stood to be preferential market access; and
(iii) liberalization occurs in 'rounds' – that is, in distinct negoti-
      ating periods with a definable beginning and end (albeit the
      'end' has become a rather elastic concept).

MFN, reciprocity and national treatment are then applied and
adjustments made thereafter to ensure 'balance'. To reiterate,

reciprocity dictates that exchanges must be roughly equivalent in value, though in a competitive system the incentive is to give away as little as possible for as much as can be achieved in return. MFN requires – certain exceptions notwithstanding – that each participant treats all others as if they were their most privileged trading partner, albeit again that the incentive is not to treat competitors as well as they treat you. National treatment requires that once inside national borders goods and services are treated in the same way as their domestic equivalents, with the caveats here being that: (i) they first have to enter domestic markets (with the incentive being to restrict highly competitive goods) and (ii) each good and service is recognized and treated as a 'like' product (which gives legislators licence to be imaginative in their classification system so that highly competitive goods and services are not treated as like products and therefore are not eligible for preferential treatment).

Organized in this way, political bargaining among states differing dramatically in terms of their capacity to negotiate, size, make-up and diversity of their economies as well as their military, ideological, material and non-material significance contributes to the production of deals that vary considerably in terms of the opportunities they confer. Inevitably the larger more economically significant states have tended to fare better than their smaller developing counterparts. As we saw in the previous chapter, early liberalization in industrial goods, for instance, proved beneficial (as had been the intent) to the United States and the European economies, whereas it was of questionable value to those developing countries that were original contracting parties to the GATT (such as Cuba, Southern Rhodesia, Burma, Sri Lanka, Brazil, Pakistan or Chile – all of which were much more interested in liberalizing areas that remained heavily protected such as agricultural and tropical produce). Differences in negotiating capacities – in terms of technical expertise; human, financial and other resources; and the capacity to establish permanent delegations in Geneva – contributed further to this imbalance. Indeed, few of the original developing-country contracting parties were adequately represented during the first GATT negotiations and several (such as Southern Rhodesia) took part in the negotiations merely as satellite states of the then colonial powers.

Yet, matters were (and are) compounded by the pursuit of liberalization in rounds. Simply put, each time a negotiation took place it did so, not in isolation, but on the basis of the outcome of the previous rounds. As D. M McRae and J. C. Thomas put it (1983: 67), 'the mechanics of negotiations . . . can only be understood against a background of previous . . . negotiating rounds conducted under the auspices of GATT'. This meant that delegations approached a new round mindful of what had gone before and of any inequities that had resulted therein. It is precisely because trade negotiations are 'iterated games' that the outcome of one necessarily affects the way future 'games' are played. This is the case for large and small countries alike.

During the Kennedy round, for example, the United States attempted to rectify what it perceived to be the relatively greater gains made by the EEC in the previous rounds (Lee, 2001). It was, as Robert Aliber put it (1970: 232), 'a reflection of the United States' "Grand Design" for Atlantic Relations'. Likewise, the Tokyo round was designed in large part to continue the unfinished business of the Kennedy round, principally in three areas – industrial goods, agriculture and 'the trade of developing countries' (McRae and Thomas, 1983: 54).

This iterated form of bargaining has, inevitably, put GATT contracting parties/WTO members at loggerheads with one another; and the development of the GATT/WTO has been such that the two groups most frequently perceived to be at loggerheads with one another – and which has most strongly contributed to the consolidation of group identities – are developing countries (as those primarily seeking to rectify past anomalies) and their industrial counterparts (as those seeking to protect sectors of decreasing competitiveness and political sensitivity as well as to open up new areas of economic opportunity). The problem is that in approaching trade negotiations, those seeking some kind of retribution are encouraged to agree to new concessions in return for remedial action. This is the logic of any bargaining-based system. Yet, it is because of this requirement to offer something in return for that which is received, coupled with existing power inequalities between participating states, that asymmetries in outcome have been perpetuated and exacerbated in successive GATT/WTO rounds. The Uruguay round – the results of which were discussed in detail in the previous chapter – provides a useful example of the exchange of concessions in new areas for remedial action.

The point here is that the use of exchange as the mechanism of liberalizing (and governing) trade among states of vastly different capabilities in institutional confines that favour the industrial states over their developing counterparts has produced bargains that are of dramatically different value to participating states (that is, they are asymmetrical). As negotiations take place in bursts over time, the inequities of one negotiation have an influence on structuring another; and, as it is only in reciprocating for concessions received that a round can hope to reach a conclusion, it is only through a process of exchange that past anomalies can be redressed. Yet, it is precisely because each exchange is asymmetrical that as negotiations take place the imbalance of opportunity among participating states is exacerbated rather than attenuated. And, while it is the case that the least developed countries are relieved of the requirement to reciprocate, this is not unproblematic primarily because – as we have seen – it excludes them from influencing in any way the shape of the negotiations. The consequence is to produce one asymmetrical bargain after another. Yet, it is only when all of the negotiations are taken as a whole – that is, over the lifetime of the institution – that the extent of this asymmetry can be appreciated; and it is only when viewed in this way that we can appreciate how entrenched the imbalance in the distribution of opportunities has become.

Attempts to accelerate progress in rounds at identified moments such as during ministerial conferences are equally problematic. Negotiating in this fashion generates an institutional culture wherein bargaining only begins with vigour in the closing stages of a meeting – the eleventh-hour negotiating that characterized the closing stages of the December 2013 Bali ministerial conference is a good example (see Wilkinson, Hannah and Scott, 2014). This culture not only creates a pressure cooker atmosphere where delegations are encouraged by the anxiety and pressure of the moment to agree to concessions that upon reflection may prove to be less than favourable, it exacerbates further the consequences of relative differences in negotiating capacities of each member state. Delegations from the least developed countries, for example, struggle not just to take a sufficient number of staff to a ministerial conference but to find personnel with a sufficient understanding of the issues to enable meaningful negotiations to take place, leaving them to rely on the technical assistance of their competitors and/or briefings from NGOs (the majority of whom are also excluded from crucial meetings) and wandering around the press/NGO centre waiting with the other gathered observers for an announcement on the state of play. As Dipak Patel famously once noted, the *Financial Times* has more people and a greater capacity to cover trade policy than he did had as Chair of the LDC group.[10]

First to the game

The problems generated by bargaining between unequals in iterated rounds in the pursuit of an exchange of concessions in highly pressured settings are compounded by the point at which a state begins to participate in the multilateral trading system. Crudely put, the earlier a state began participating in the GATT/WTO, the more able it was to influence the shape of negotiations and the less likely it was to have to accept overly burdensome membership requirements (particularly since the creation of the WTO). This is Keohane's (2002: 253) point about 'first' – and we might add 'early' – mover advantages. This was clearly the case with the GATT. The GATT was designed around the needs of its principal architects and excluded those areas that were strategically important and in which liberalization would have been beneficial to new entrants. Those industrial states that had chosen not to participate at the institution's inception acceded to the *General Agreement* soon thereafter so that by the mid 1950s all of the major industrial trading nations were signatories. Few had economic and geostrategic interests that differed from the kind of programme of liberalization that was put in place by the institution's architects. Most sought the freeing up of trade in manufactures, semi-manufactures and capital goods while protecting their agricultural markets. Thus, their interests were largely served by the way the GATT was constructed and the manner in which liberalization was pursued.

Thereafter, the accession of non-industrial countries was relatively automatic. Many newly independent states were sponsored by their former colonial powers – so-called 'grand-fathering'. These states did not accede, however, on terms of their own making. They were often presented with GATT accession as a fait accompli (Basra, 2012). Their interests were seldom represented and their role in GATT negotiations was often limited. Others had accession processes that were a little more drawn out but which, nonetheless, ensured they acceded to the GATT in a distinctly disadvantageous way. Japan's accession was perhaps the most extreme in this regard (Patterson, 1966: 272–300).

During the Uruguay round many countries were encouraged to sign up to the GATT to bypass the more demanding regime that would emerge under the WTO. The rush that ensued ensured that detailed assessments of the consequences of accession were often overlooked or simply ignored (Lanoszka, 2001). Those who have acceded since have had to agree to ever more demanding accession protocols requiring significant domestic economic adjustments without being able to demand the same kind of reciprocation of already existing members (of which China's accession is a good example – see Scott and Wilkinson, 2013a: 768–71).

The point here is that the entry of states into the trade regime has been heavily policed since the GATT was first agreed. New entrants were either (i) 'grandfathered' into the system (if they were deemed to be of little economic and political significance and threat, and/or were the former colonies of the European powers) during the institution's early years; (ii) faced with a barrage of exception actions that nullified most of the benefits of membership (as was Japan's experience after its 1955 accession); and/or (iii) required to agree to significant and overly burdensome protocols that went far beyond what was required of existing members (as in the case of China's accession, but also that of the least developed small island state of Vanuatu – see Hayashi 2003; WTO 2012b). Indeed, what is quite clear is that the accession requirements have become steadily more, rather than less, demanding over the institution's life cycle (Copelovitch and Ohls, 2012; also UNCTAD 2001).

It thus remains the case that the shape of the system, both in terms of the rules adopted and the liberalization pursued, was primarily tailored to the needs of the institution's architects and few changes to (or indeed opportunities to change) the system have occurred since it was first negotiated. Those countries that acceded at the outset were more able to influence the shape of negotiations and the manner in which the institution evolved; whereas later entrants have had to be largely accepting of the manner in which trade is liberalized as well as, for those joining under WTO rules, of the requirements made of them. Needless to say, this has contributed to the imbalance in the distribution of economic opportunities arising from GATT/WTO accession. It has also ensured that the current accession regime has become a point of focus for reform.

Mini-lateralism in a multilateral setting

Even more problematic is the continuation of the practice of a small number of states dominating negotiations. Since the GATT was first negotiated, the core of the negotiations has always taken place between and among the most significant trading nations (even the original negotiations, nominally among 23 contracting parties, were conducted primarily between the United States and the United Kingdom). In the early years this 'mini-lateralism' was institutionalized through the use of the principal supplier rule (discussed in detail in the previous chapter). More recently, it has been manifest in the striking of bargains among the most significant trading nations, whether that is the United States and European Union (the G2), the 'Quad' (United States, European Union, Japan and Canada), the new G4 (India, China, United States and European Union), the Five Interested Parties (G4 plus Australia) and so on.

Arranged in this way, negotiations often see agreements hammered out among small groups and then multilateralized to the wider membership (who, depending on their developmental status, are then either obliged to reciprocate or else get some measure of relief). This ensures some states (the ones at the core) are able to negotiate and agree an exchange of concessions that are meaningful, while others (those peripheralized by the process) can only say 'yes' or 'no' to a broad swathe of unspecific measures designed to encourage their acceptance of a grand bargain under a single undertaking.

Allied to this small group – what is known as 'green room'[11] – diplomacy are other practices designed to forge agreement. Recent negotiations have seen the emergence of 'confessionals' to reveal delegations' bottom lines, the appointment of 'friends of the chair', and various 'forum-plus' tactics such as strong-arming delegates, linkage to non-trade (particularly security) concerns and the like (Narlikar and Wilkinson, 2004). These practices have been widely decried (see, for instance, Jawara and Kwa, 2003). Nevertheless, they have contributed to the production of asymmetrical bargains. Moreover, they have provided a focus of attention for calls for reforming the WTO.

Single undertaking, double jeopardy

The use of an exchange of concessions as the basis upon which trade opportunities are realized has created further problems. During the GATT years states unwilling, or unable, simply opted out of agreeing to the final bargain. While this meant that in so doing they also reduced their capacity to have a say in the shape and direction of the GATT (Wilkinson and Scott, 2008), it nevertheless cushioned them from making certain concessions. However, the capacity to opt out was removed during the Uruguay round with the introduction of the single undertaking – that is, the agreement that all participants are bound by all agreements (the previous Tokyo round had also sought its introduction, though, rather ironically, the à la carte system of plurilateral agreements that emerged therefrom was quite the opposite and has come back into fashion of late – about which more is said below).

The introduction of a single undertaking has had several consequences. It has encouraged all participants to take an interest in the negotiations as all are required to be bound by its outcome. This, in turn, has produced greater energy around negotiating itself which has made the conclusion of deals more difficult (as the Doha round, and Uruguay before it, show) as well as further illuminated the vast differences that exist in the technical capacity of delegations. However, the pursuit of a single undertaking also brings with it a tendency towards perpetual asymmetry. Without the capacity to opt out, the losers of any previous trade deal are encouraged to agree to further movement forward in exchange for remedial measures. A good example of this is the agreement to movement forward in trade facilitation in exchange for minor concessions on food security and an LDC package at the Bali ministerial conference. Inevitably this ensures that the gulf between the economic opportunities offered to participants by trade deals will at least remain, if not increase, with the conclusion of each round (particularly because those economic interests that are able to exploit new market openings first will accrue significant advantages from doing so). For developing countries this is a case of damned if they are part of a single undertaking and damned if they are not. It also underlines clearly why competitive negotiations are an inappropriate way to generate outcomes that, in turn, govern global trade.

What happens when unequals bargain

The consequences of bargaining among unequals in these confines have not been limited to the production of asymmetrical bargains alone. It has also, inevitably, produced a particular kind of politics, one in which heightened contestation and drama feature predominantly. This is unsurprising particularly as the WTO functions in much the same way the GATT did more than half a century ago. As Harry Johnson argued 'the real trouble with GATT . . . [is] the techniques of bargaining and especially the procedure of bargaining between dominant suppliers on a basis of bilateral balancing'. These techniques belong 'to the 1930s' and not to the present day (Johnson, 1968: 368; also Hudec, 1990: 57). Given that the trade regime has been constructed in this way and that no substantive reform has been attempted or undertaken since its creation it is no surprise that trade politics should have become so contested.

This heightened contestation has a number of consequences of which three are noteworthy here. First, it has produced a form of alliance bargaining that has sought to overcome the structural impediments and blockages to deals that have emerged. Coalitions have been a feature of the GATT since the 1960s and they have consistently been used by developing countries in an attempt to gain greater leverage in negotiations. For instance, in the early 1960s Nigeria led a group of 21 developing countries in proposing a programme of action urging the contracting parties as a whole (and the industrial states particularly) to focus their negotiating attentions on targeting barriers to trade identified as directly affecting the 'less-developed' states (GATT, 1963: 204–6).[12] What is notable about the Nigerian-led coalition is that it was put together precisely to overcome the exclusion that it and the 20 other countries had suffered during the Dillon round (1960–1). This kind of alliance politics also appeared during the subsequent Kennedy round and was again used as a means of trying to leverage issues of developing-country concern into the mainstream of the negotiations. Indeed, if it had not been for initiatives such as these (and threats to leave the system in favour of what was originally intended to be an alternative institution in the form of UNCTAD), it is unlikely that any development-friendly modifications would have been made to the GATT (such as Part IV).

What is striking about the emergence of coalition politics in the GATT/WTO is not simply the way it has ballooned as a developing-country strategy – witness the creation of the G20, G33, G90 and G110 among others during the Doha round – but that it has also become a tool used by industrial states (see Narlikar, 2003; Narlikar and Tussie, 2004 for extended commentaries). What is also notable is that certain coalitions have become semi-permanent features of multilateral trade politics irrespective of whether their significance has waxed and waned over time.

Second, the strategic deployment of the GATT/WTO, the differentials in size and shape of the member countries, and the institutional format in which they interact has produced a form of politics that is predicated on bluff and brinkmanship and which has become increasingly defined by moments of crisis and collapse. Much like coalition politics, this has been a long-standing feature of the trade negotiations. It was a strong feature of the ITO negotiations; crisis, collapse and brinkmanship almost scuppered the first round of GATT negotiations (see Wilkinson, 2006a: 31–2); and it has been a feature of all of the WTO's ministerial conferences at which negotiations have been attempted (particularly Cancún, Hong Kong and Bali). Seasoned observers and trade negotiators know this pattern well and use it to their advantage. Those less familiar with the patter of trade negotiations – particularly those developing countries that have little technical capacity and whose representatives do not often remain in post for long periods of time – are less attuned to the drama that comes with rounds. Former Canadian trade negotiator Sylvia Ostry's view is that it takes about a decade to become well versed in the art of trade negotiations and to be able to see these kinds of tactics for what they are.[13]

What is also notable is that whereas brinkmanship and crisis engineering were effective in encouraging forward momentum historically, as developing countries have built up their technical capacity and knowledge base not only of the content of what is at stake but also how negotiations are conducted, these tactics have begun to lose traction. It is, for instance, hard to see how a US-manipulated collapse of a ministerial conference – as occurred in Cancún in 2003 (Bhagwati, 2004) – could be repeated with the same effect now (that is, bringing disaffected parties back to the table, even if this inevitably lasted only until the next collapse).

As the tactical traction of brinkmanship and crisis engineering has lessened the focus has shifted to a third form of behaviour: the use of bilateral, regional and plurilateral levers as devices for encouraging forward momentum at moments of intransigence. Again, this has always been a feature of trade politics. What is notable is that when rounds become deadlocked a resort to the politics of mini-lateralism is used as the vehicle deployed to get negotiations back on track. As we noted earlier, the creation of NAFTA was in part a levering device over the European Community. The TPP and TTIP negotiations are equally of this ilk (though this time it is the BRICS rather than the EC that are the targets of US mini-lateralism). What is also noteworthy is how the pulse of the knowledge community circling round trade negotiations has latched onto the idea of mini-lateral agreements (bilateral, plurilateral, regional) as the best-case scenario in the face of a failing round irrespective of the clear fact that it is not, and never has been, in the interests of the major players to abandon the multilateral game. As former USTR Susan Schwab openly acknowledges, bilateralism and regionalism are only ever strategic devices in a greater multilateral game (Schwab, 2009; see also da Conceição-Heldt, 2014).

Conclusion

What we have then is a system that produces unfair outcomes and which does so because it pitches states of dramatically different size and capacity against one another in an institutional confine that favours the industrial countries as the institution's architects and early joiners. Moreover, we see that in the absence of a fundamental overhaul, the differences in member capability and the form and content of WTO rules ensures that asymmetrical bargains will continue to be produced. In the face of continued and compounded inequity, the inevitable result has been increased belligerence and to render the multilateral trading system deadlocked. Certainly other parts of the system continue to function – notably, but not uncontroversially, the dispute settlement mechanism and the trade policy review mechanism. Most certainly the secretariat has been hard at work trying to keep the system going by generating an ever greater number of tasks for itself as well as actually trying to take the politics out of ministerial conferences and WTO public forums. Yet, unless something dramatic is done that enables the system to generate different bargains, and to do so by means other than competition, the system will continue to falter.

That said, the blockages to WTO reform are not merely institutional. Nor are they forged out of the habit engendered by the persistent use of a system that favours the interests of the few over those of the many. They are also intellectual and ideational. We are as path dependent in our thinking about trade as the WTO is in the way it governs trade. Thus, before we can think seriously and differently about how we reform the institution we first need to pay attention to the way we think and talk about trade. It is to this subject that the next chapter turns.

CHAPTER THREE

Talking trade

The way we talk about trade is unique. It is unique because, unlike any other area of economic and political debate, conversations often distil complex arguments into easily consumable ways of talking. These ways of talking – commonly taking the form of the metaphorical sound bites and, less frequently, more involved but nonetheless stylized historical accounts – present those reading or listening with snippets of logic that convey a subjective position about how the world works. At the same time they often portray opponents of free trade in highly unflattering ways designed to undermine their credibility using what we imagine is 'common-sense' logic – George W. Bush's remark that we should 'make no mistake [that] those who protest free trade are no friends of the poor' (cited in Stanley and Hoge, 2001) functions in precisely this fashion. Thomas Friedman's (1999) question: 'Is there anything more ridiculous in the news today then the protests against the World Trade Organization in Seattle?' His answer that, 'I doubt it. These anti-WTO protesters . . . are a Noah's ark of flat-earth advocates, protectionist trade unions and yuppies looking for their 1960s fix', does likewise. Jagdish Bhagwati's assertion that free trade's opponents are 'the chaff' that needs separating from 'the wheat' of good sense, and that '[s]adly, the critics who are most off the mark, and indeed off the wall, are to be found among the well-meaning non-governmental organizations' (2005: 25) is similar in vein.

We have become so consumed with stylized ways of talk-ing about trade and accepting of the insults thrown that we are unable to see that these forms of communicating blind us to the strategic manner in which the GATT/WTO has been deployed and the asymmetrical outcomes its liberalization has produced. Moreover, we fail to see that they distract our attention sufficiently to maintain the illusion that equitable trade outcomes can be negotiated by bargaining among unequals in loaded places. Equally, we fail to realize that these subjective positions are presented as if they were true 'facts' and their biases – ideological, interest-wise or other – are hidden behind the logic of a metaphor, an historical account, a constructed identity and/or the commonsense logic (that we might just be able to 'level the playing field' or harvest 'low-hanging fruit') with which the reader or listener is presented.

The problems here are two-fold. The presentation of metaphor, historical logic or constructed identity as fact and commonsense simultaneously encourages (i) particular forms of behaviour while at the same time (ii) safeguarding that logic from critical scrutiny. Much like our reluctance to ask fundamental questions about the way multilateral liberalization has been conducted and the appropriateness of bargaining among unequals in institutional confines that clearly favour the industrial states, our acceptance of these ways of talking about trade as the way we converse with one another constrains us not only from asking questions about where we are going but also having debates about the future of trade and its governance that are genuinely 'outside the box'.

If we are to reform the existing system – perhaps even install a new one – we need to recognize that the problems that exist are more than the way the GATT/WTO was deployed and designed. We need to change fundamentally the way we think and talk about trade. We need to move beyond simply regurgitating received wisdom about trade – as George Orwell noted we need to resist using language without thinking, and repeating words and phrases simply because their use has become habit

(Orwell, [1946] 1962). We need to subject to critical interrogation the meanings underpinning (and often obscured by) the way we speak and the language we use. And we need to filter out the forms of behaviour that preclude others from engaging in genuine conversations about trade.

The aim of this chapter is to show how the way that we talk about trade affects the way we think and act which, in turn, has an effect on how we think about the institution's reform. My purpose is to get us to think about the way we talk and listen to arguments about trade so that we no longer take commonsense wisdom at face value and are not persuaded by simple assertions that trade is like a 'bicycle' and needs to be kept in perpetual motion, that the world economy will collapse if further liberalization is not pursued and/or trade 'gains' rolled back, that 'rising tides will lift all boats', that the WTO is not a development organization, that free-riders (a label more often than not attached to developing countries) necessarily are free-riding or that using insults as discursive devices is an appropriate way to behave. Put simply, the chapter is intended to get us to think twice about the value of what we take to be commonsense trade logic.

The chapter begins by examining how the metaphorical and historical devices as well as the constructed identities we deploy when thinking and talking about trade bind us into unhelpful intellectual circuits from which we struggle to extract ourselves. It then examines how the way we talk about trade can have an impact on encouraging forward momentum at moments of intransigence, making the production of asymmetrical bargains more, rather than less likely. It explores the tensions between, on the one hand the pursuit of freer trade as an inalienable good in itself, and on the other hand, claims that the WTO is not a development organization. And it points to those new frontiers that have opened up in the way we talk about trade but which do little to move us beyond existing commonsense wisdom. The chapter concludes by showing how the way that we currently talk about trade forces us to think inside the box at a moment when we need to do just the opposite.

It's all commonsense, right?

One way language contributes to the maintenance of particular relations of power is through the dissemination of 'commonsense' – what we think of as those words and phrases that convey everyday wisdom, what we all ought to know, what is obvious, and what is in front of one's nose (as Orwell put it in 1946).[14] As Antonio Gramsci remarked, commonsense is the 'traditional popular conception of the world' (Gramsci, 1998: 198–9), that which is instinctive, rarely questioned, or subject to critical scrutiny (Fairclough, 2001: 64). Yet, it is not just 'wisdom' and 'knowledge' that commonsense conveys; it also suggests particular kinds of behaviour that we assume are, or must be, appropriate (Fairclough, 2001: 64).

Commonsense is particularly important in understanding how language contributes to the perpetuation of particular ideas held to be 'right' and their relationship to specific relations of power. Precisely because commonsense is held to be 'true' or 'fact' it is seldom challenged. It nevertheless suggests modes of behaviour that are consistent with the ideas and ideologies that underpin a social order. In so doing, commonsense helps shape what it is that we deem to be politically possible. Other forms of wisdom and attendant modes of behaviour – ones that may or may not be equally or more appropriate – are either obscured from view, dismissed as non-commonsensical or else they are rendered plain false. Moreover, the penalties can be sufficiently high to militate against challenging commonsense (as the story of Socrates and his demise poignantly illustrates – see de Botton, 2000: 14–42). Yet, it is precisely because commonsense embodies assumptions that treat authority and hierarchy as natural, reflect the wisdom of dominant ideologies (Fairclough, 2001: 2) and presuppose that particular courses of action or modes of behaviour are the most appropriate (Gramsci, 1998: 348–50) that it needs to be challenged.

Metaphors play an important role in conveying commonsense. They help create social realities, construct ideas of what is 'true' and 'false', and specify particular kinds of action (see Lakoff and Johnson, 1980). Metaphors can also change the way events are perceived and understood, thereby altering conceptions of what is deemed to be 'true', prescribing particular courses of action while crowding out or delegitimizing others. This is done by replacing an act, event, instance or attribute with a word or phrase that conveys a particular meaning intended to underline or alter perceptions such that they serve a set of interests. Medical metaphors, for instance, are often used in political discourse to underline the dangers of particular ideologies or courses of action as well as to celebrate others (see Sontag, 2002). During the Cold War, for example, the use of the word 'cancer' in association with the spread of communism served not only to reinforce negative perceptions of communism, it also prescribed (and legitimized) practices consistent with halting its spread (Hook, 1984: 262). As Glenn Hook explains, the use of the metaphor in this way 'helps to structure reality by *locating* an issue in a certain *context* calling forth certain *entailments*' (Hook, 1984: 263, emphasis in the original).

The words, metaphors, phrases and linguistic constructions that convey commonsense form part of a wider discourse. Discourses are organic aspects of any social order. They emerge out of particular historical moments and change with, are reproduced by and influence the shape of the orders from which they emerge. They create exclusionary arenas (locking in some kinds of wisdom while crowding out others) empowering particular individuals to speak. Those who have been assimilated into, learnt or have been socialized by a dominant discourse and who use it in communicating (verbally, in writing or otherwise) are 'heard', while those who do not use the discourse, or are excluded by it, are silenced. Moreover, discourses are seldom static. They are reproduced and mutate through usage as well as change in response to challenges both to their credibility as well as to underlying ideas and interests. They also notably intensify at some moments and fall into relative abeyance at others. In so doing, they assist in perpetuating their underlying interests and relations of power.

What we know, then, is that language can shape behaviour. We know that language develops and is deployed in a wider social context. As such, it reflects those hierarchies and power relationships that are prevalent at any given moment in time. We know that behaviour is shaped not just through direct instructions, but also by the received wisdom embodied in commonsense (whether it is through stock phrases, metaphors or other linguistic constructions). We know that the use of a particular language creates some possibilities for action (consistent with the ideas and interests that underpin a discourse) while crowding out others. We know that it matters who speaks; and that by speaking, which voices are heard. We know that at moments wherein threats to the interests and power relationships underpinning a discourse emerge, an intensification and/or subtle (and sometimes dramatic) changes in the substance of a discourse can result. It is with these conceptual markers in mind that we now turn to the forms and functions of how we think and speak about multilateral trade.

Pestilence, history, villains and who to blame

The relationship between trade and war is one area wherein metaphors and pithy accounts purporting to be accurate historical renditions are presented in ways that overly simplify the complex relationship between commerce and conflict (see Bearce and Fisher, 2002). The key to this form of argumentation is the use of metaphorical and/or distilled examples where the logic of the story illustrates clearly the necessity of taking one course of action over another. In early twentieth century – particularly post-First World War – accounts seeking to associate freer trade with the pursuit of world peace, stylized and abstracted stories were common. Demonstrating clearly the utility of metaphorical argument in presenting his case for freer trade, J. Russell Smith used the fixing of a broken sewage pipe to stem a typhoid outbreak as a proxy for the necessity of addressing the root causes of war (of which freer trade was a necessary component) and the primary care given to patients by hospital nurses as a synonym for the hopelessness of treating the symptoms of war once it had broken out (Smith, 1919: 287). This form of argumentation was also prevalent in the immediate post-Second World War era. Here commentators such as Clair Wilcox crafted their case for freer trade using metaphorical and stylized historical argument to support commonsense messages. While Wilcox also used disease as a metaphor, his work also drew on the selective presentation of the passage of world events in the preceding 150 years as a resource to warn of the economic destitution and political extremism that would result if liberalization was not pursued (Wilcox, 1949a: 3–10, 12–13).

Aside from its historical one-dimensionality, what is interesting about Wilcox's account – and others like it – is his blindness to the falsities and illogic of his own argument. His claim that the century immediately preceding the First World War as one of peace and stability (Wilcox, 1949a: 3) sketches over significant conflicts and ignores successive periods of imperial aggrandisement, uprisings, civil wars and rebellions engulfing, among many other countries, Italy, Greece, Germany, Portugal, Poland, France, the United States, Hungary, Austria, China, Afghanistan, Turkey, Thailand, Hawaii, Peru, Chile, Colombia, Ethiopia, Morocco, Russia, Central Asia, Mexico, Brazil, Uganda, South Africa and Armenia. Likewise, Wilcox's claim that the century prior to the

First World War had been one where goods moved with relative freedom is not unproblematic. British agriculture was heavily protected until the repeal of the Corn Laws (in 1846) and restrictions remained thereafter. Agricultural protectionism was a key feature of the German and Swedish economies in the late nineteenth century. Britain, France and Germany routinely protected their infant industries. Tariffs in the United States were consistently and uniformly high (Irwin, 2001) and foreign investment in banking, shipping, mining and logging was strictly regulated (Chang, 2007). Moreover, the United States, Britain, Germany and France regularly allowed copyrights and patents to be floated (even explicitly allowing the production of counterfeit goods) (see Accominotti and Flandreau, 2008 for further commentary).

Yet it is not just what Wilcox said that is important, it is who he was. It is precisely because of his role in the American polity and academy that this version of events gained credibility. Wilcox was a professor in the Economics Department (and, for 37 years, its Chair) at Swarthmore College (1927–68). He co-authored (with Paul H. Douglas – a University of Chicago economist and later Democratic Senator for Illinois – another key public intellectual) a petition against the 1930 Smoot-Hawley tariff (signed by 1,028 economists). He led the Office of International Trade Policy at the State Department from 1945–8 (the competencies of which were later transferred over to form part of the interagency Office of the US Trade Representative, USTR, as it became, in 1962). He was head of the US delegation to the London Conference on the Charter for the ITO. And he was vice-chairman of the US delegation to the Havana Conference on Trade and Employment (which concluded the ITO Charter).

Others too were also instrumental in putting forward these commonsense messages, such as University of Chicago and Princeton Economics Professor and sometime advisor to the US Treasury Jacob Viner; William Adams Brown, a contemporary of Wilcox's during the ITO negotiations and at Swarthmore;

Wilcox's student and Council on Foreign Relations stalwart William Diebold Jr; and Cambridge Professor, Director of the Bank of England and co-author of the Bretton Woods system John Maynard Keynes (see Viner, 1947; Brown, 1950; Diebold, 1952; Keynes, 1946).

In arguing their case, what Wilcox, Viner, Brown, Diebold, Keynes and others did was help put in place a core story that warned against the follies of not liberalizing trade married to a strong vision of what would transpire should this logic not be followed. This story was then disseminated domestically (particularly within the United States) and internationally which, in turn, helped secure the necessary support for multilateral trade liberalization to begin under the GATT. And it served to frame a particular kind of liberalization that simultaneously opened up trade in particular areas of importance to the United States, while protecting others.

These liberalization-cum-war arguments have not been confined to the annals of history, however. They resurface in more contemporary (and rather hyperbolic) accounts worrying about the future of the multilateral trading system. Again, what is common to all is a form of historical reductionism that grooms the 'lessons' of history in ways that are permissive to the arguments being pursued. As Gabriel Siles-Brügge (2013: 4) puts it, they create 'an ideational imperative . . . by drawing on a questionable reading of economic history'.

Three points about the way these arguments are manifest contemporarily are worth dwelling on here – which are then picked up on throughout the remainder of this chapter. The first is the use of catastrophe as a mechanism for driving a point home, encouraging the recipient of that wisdom to act with expediency. The second is the unique way that – more than any other challenger before – China is constructed as a threat, a state which for many has such potential that it will inevitably challenge the existing system (see Breslin, 2013 for an extended discussion). An important component of this threat construction is to eschew any evidence to the contrary and to argue that China is playing what Martin Wolf (2013) argues is a long game. As he puts it, 'China is a terrific rule follower . . . [but] I am convinced that China is playing a very very long game in a system that it intends in the long term to dominate' (Wolf, 2013). Third, all of these accounts rely on their capacity to identify a foe easily. In the early literature, the foes were identifiable as reactionary, mercantilist, anti-free trade forces. These forms of identification persist but more often than not they have moved from unidentifiable faces and shady political movements to nameable foes. This most commonly takes the form of laying blame in a highly predictable game of upstaging that unfolds after each hiccup in a trade round. The pattern is familiar to all. An agreement cannot be reached – often because it was impossible from the outset – and the countries deemed to have been the blockers to any deal are widely harangued. This haranguing goes largely uncommented upon, however.

What is worrying is that we come to acknowledge, even accept it when those being blamed are our favourite villains – favourites because we deplore their continued protection of agricultural markets, their strong-arm tactics, their neo-imperialist ways, or their domestic political structures – irrespective of whether domestic or other considerations meant a deal was never likely. We sometimes turn a blind eye when situations are engineered to collapse so that a foe can be identified for political purchase (as China was after the July 2008 mini-ministerial collapse over the Special Safeguard Mechanism, SSM – see Dresner, 2014: 349; for a rebuttal see Scott and Wilkinson, 2013a: 775–7). Yet we almost never comment when the individuals identified are labelled 'free-riders'. This is the ultimate *faux pas*.

All for nothing

The accusation that a member is accruing benefits without contribution (that is, free-riding) renders us unable to see that this label has often been used for political purposes – particularly with regard to developing countries. Sometimes it is levelled at developing countries in what is imagined as a benign fashion – they matter little in terms of their overall contribution to world trade so their lack of reciprocity also does not matter. Or else, it is deployed with more intent – to highlight a lack of contribution. Joseph Stiglitz and Andrew Charlton claim that '[a]fter effectively sitting out the first four decades of multilateral trade negotiations, developing countries' participation in the Uruguay Round led them to accept substantial liberalization of their trade regimes' (2013: 3) is an example of the former. Reducing GATT/WTO participation to activity in trade negotiations alone and developing theoretical models designed to show that the application of the most-favoured-nation clause generates a 'free-rider problem' (see, for instance, Ludema and Mayda, 2009) is an example of the latter.

Whether stated passively or more intentionally both forms of expression reinforce the commonsense logic that the largest trading countries – that is, the 'principal suppliers' – distribute benefits which are then accrued by smaller, less able states without reciprocation. What matters here is less the fact that – contrary to existing wisdom (see Maswood and Crump, 2007: 1) – the historical record shows that developing countries have actually always been actively engaged in the multilateral trading system (Wilkinson and Scott, 2008) and are structurally disadvantaged from participating fully in negotiations (both by institutional factors as well as their own economic complexion, as the two previous chapters discussed – see also Jones, 2013: 1; Jawara and Kwa, 2003), and more that the brandishing of the term 'free-rider' conjures up notions of states not pulling their weight while at the same time celebrating the contribution of non-free-riders (who just happen to be the principal beneficiaries of the trade regime).

Irrespective of its intent, and like all aspects of the 'blame

game', these accusations are unhelpful. In any social environment the levelling of blame, particularly if it is done repeatedly,
generates resentment. This, in turn, can lead to a hardening of
positions, disaffection or worse; all of which are entirely unhelpful in moving negotiations forward. Moreover, because of the
uncritical way we treat accusations of foe and free-rider we often
gloss over the very real reasons why such a set of circumstances
has come about. As with the rest of the way we talk about trade, we
need to look beneath the words and phrases that are commonly
deployed – what Orwell suggested were *'phrases* tacked together
like the sections of a prefabricated henhouse' ([1946] 1962: 145
emphasis in original) – to understand the consequences of talking in the way that we do.

Infants and insults

A more worrying trend in the way we talk about trade concerns
the tendency of some commentators to infantilize opponents to
undermine their arguments (thus presenting them as naive and
immature), to construct developing countries as if they were at
some early stage of childlike development and thus requiring the
instruction of a well-meaning parent, and to dismiss the arguments of critics in ungenerous ways – a tendency that becomes
more pronounced at pressure points in negotiations. As with
many other metaphorical expressions, these ways of talking are
unhelpful and belie ideological dispositions but are nevertheless
presented as commonsense. Developing countries are no more
like children, or their citizens infant-like, than advanced industrial countries are mature adults and appropriately qualified
parents. Certainly there is a dramatic gulf in knowledge between
industrial and developing countries and a pressing need for its
transfer, but to belittle some countries and their populations in
this way is at best inappropriate.

   Bhagwati is among those to deploy some of these techniques in
advancing his case for free trade. He writes:

> The protection of infant industries against imports much too often tends to be indiscriminate and creates strong incentives for the infant producers to remain inefficient and to continue demanding protection which then becomes politically difficult to remove. The result is that the infant does not learn and grows up wearing protectionist diapers into premature senility. (2005: 26–7)

While Bhagwati is clearly trying to use the language of infant industries as the basis for developing his argument, it is an unfortunate choice of metaphors. The assertion is that those states and commentators that advocate the protection of infant industries are resigning developing countries to a fate of perpetual infancy (whether they physically age – as the image of a diaper-wearing senile adult invokes – or not). This is designed both to ridicule opponents and to present development as a linear process to maturity. The point here is that these are not helpful ways of talking. Development is a complex process and not one that is akin to the human life cycle. And ridiculing opponents – as Bhagwati, Friedman and others on occasion do – is not an act that helps create an arena in which genuine debate can take place. What Bhagwati and others are doing is smuggling in ideological positions via metaphorical argument without being open and honest about those positions or their essentially contested nature.

Of boats, bicycles and other dramatic catastrophes

The metaphorical repertoire of trade politics is uniquely and peculiarly replete. Precisely because liberalization requires movement and freer trade is constructed as forward progress from more restricted trade (and unenlightened times), WTO politics is laden with metaphors of motion occasionally mixed in with ideas of natural forces and phenomena. The idea that liberalization will be a tide that 'lifts all boats' (see Hines, Hoynes and Krueger, 2001; Berg and Krueger, 2007) is one such instance that is both natural and rather gentle in the vision it evokes; the use of 'sunshine' as a metaphor for transparency in the WTO's dispute settlement system is another (Wolfe, 2014). The use of a train, and in particular the necessity of keeping it firmly on its rails lest it crash (with catastrophic consequences), is a more dramatic construction (see Heydon, 2006; Drache, 2006).

As we have seen, the highly political nature of the GATT, the manner in which the institution evolved and the pitching of unequals together in adversarial negotiations ensured that trade negotiations were, from the very outset, highly contested affairs. The drama that ensued imbued negotiations with a propensity to crisis and, on occasion, collapse. These moments of drama were taken seriously, particularly as they threatened to undermine the institution and the purpose for which it had been designed. They also threatened to undermine the case for further liberalization. The result was that worries about what might result if liberalization should be allowed to stall continually framed GATT negotiations, and the case was made repeatedly at moments when the institution appeared to be in crisis. What emerged – as we saw in the more historical accounts discussed above – was a 'crisis discourse', one that encouraged a particular kind of political behaviour by framing trade negotiations in a manner consistent with the conclusion of bargains by warning against what might transpire should the process of multilateral trade liberalization be interrupted (see Wilkinson, 2009).

What is interesting about this crisis discourse is that, not only has it become a key part of the commonsense history of the GATT, it has come to be expressed metaphorically. As we have seen, metaphors were deployed from the very outset. Yet, one has proven unique and tenacious: the bicycle. At its simplest, the bicycle suggests that trade liberalization, like the forward motion required to keep a bicycle moving, needs to be in a state of perpetual motion. If that motion were to cease, the process (like the bicycle) would collapse and cause injury to the global economy/

the bicycle's rider. The use of this metaphor serves, at one and the same time, to simplify, clarify and intensify the mental image constructed by the crisis discourse of what would happen if the multilateral process were allowed to stall despite the self-evident fact that the trading system is very unlike a bicycle or its movement linear in the way the metaphor would encourage us to believe. Moreover, it creates an imperative around the perpetuation of a particular kind of trade liberalization – one that, as we have seen, primarily benefited core interests while at the same time offering only limited prospects to those on the periphery – that has resulted in the conclusion of successive trade bargains that have been deeply asymmetrical.

It is no mistake that the bicycle metaphor emerged as serious impediments to further liberalization began to emerge in the late 1960s and early 1970s. By this point, GATT negotiations had become progressively harder to conclude because of increases in the number of contracting parties (which posed logistical as well as political problems especially because of the growing militancy of newly independent states), the growing depth and extent of the trade agenda, mounting tensions between the then European Economic Community and the United States and growing protectionist sentiment in both, a worsening international economic environment, and mounting concern among developing countries that their interests were not being served (see Ibrahim, 1978).

Attributed to C. Fred Bergsten,[15] the bicycle metaphor conveyed the message of the lengthier and more involved core story put forward by Wilcox and others to a domestic US and international public and polity that was nearly thirty years removed from the end of the Second World War, nearly forty years from the inter-war depression, and had enjoyed (at least in the United States) two decades of unrivalled prosperity. It did not require recipients of this received wisdom to understand the intricacies of what had caused the depression, but the necessity of maintaining forward motion sought to encourage support for further liberalization. In so doing it made commonsense of the notion that unless the trade bicycle continually moved forward it would topple over. As Bergsten put it, the '[s]teady movement toward trade liberalization is necessary to halt the acceleration of the trend toward increasing trade restrictions' (Bergsten, 1973: 280).

Since they were first articulated, a consensus has emerged around the logic of the crisis discourse and the bicycle metaphor. Both have become staples of trade politics and are widely known and frequently used. Moreover, in that process wherein subjective views are assimilated as social truths, the metaphor has itself been elevated to the status of both 'theory' and 'fact'. As James Bacchus, former chair of the WTO's appellate body, puts it, '[a]ccording to the "bicycle theory," the history of trade, and of trade policymaking, teaches us that a failure to move steadily forward toward freer trade condemns the world trading system to topple over' (Bacchus, 2003: 429).

As the Doha round negotiations have progressed and the talks have ground to a seemingly intractable halt, subtle changes in the content of the crisis discourse have occurred. These changes are neither unheard of nor are unprecedented. Rather, they are consistent with other intensifications that have occurred across the life of the trade regime. On occasion this intensification appears passive – such as WTO DG Roberto Azevêdo's pre-Bali ministerial conference appeal, echoing similar calls made by each of the three previous DGs (Wilkinson, 2009: 606–12) to members to bear in mind that what is 'at stake is the credibility of the multilateral trading system itself' (WTO, 2013a). It can also be much more active and aggressive, as the use of a dramatic and high-stakes language on the state of the round, and the plight of the organization, illustrates. The life-and-death terms in which Jagdish Bhagwati presents the pre-Bali WTO is a prime example (CUTS, 2013).

What is notable about this more active and aggressive turn in language is that all too often the state of the round is presented in life and death terms, with commentators competing to be the first to proclaim Doha 'dead' (and to write *the* obituary – see Kleimann and Guinan, 2011), or else suggesting that with enough energy the round's impending demise could be averted. In many cases, this life-and-death struggle is sharpened with the use of other metaphors. These metaphors are often medical, such as likening the state of the round to a 'coma' or else encouraging us to imagine that it is on 'life support', though other metaphors are also used. The point here is that, once deployed, these metaphors are then taken to their logical conclusion to reinforce the need to pursue a particular course of action, such as to accept the round's failure and let the patient 'die', drum up support for dramatic intervention (such as 'surgery', 'amputation', 'chemical correction') to salvage the negotiations, or else engage in a spot of 'euthanasia' or a distasteful, but nonetheless necessary, 'assassination' (Harbinson, 2011).

The problem with talking in such dramatic ways is that it presupposes and necessitates that quite dramatic action *is* necessary. In so doing, it hooks readers into a form of argumentation that suggests that only a particular course of action consistent with the commentator's predisposition is worth pursuing. This, in turn, limits discussion to those options associated with a diagnosis that sees the situation as chronic and the solution as dramatic. The issue here is that the use of such high-stakes language crowds out discussion of solutions that are *not* dramatic and which *do not* speak to the solutions proposed by the original commentator. Hence, the momentum of the bicycle must be maintained; the train must be prevented from coming off the rails; and a patient in terminal decline must either be treated immediately and robustly or else put out of his or her misery.

The point here is that the entailments that accompany a metaphor, or for that matter the manner about which a subject is spoken, set the boundaries of what is understood to be politically possible. The message is clear: bridge the divides and conclude the round, or else the breakdown of the multilateral trading system and something akin to the nightmare of the 1930s will be upon us. Yet, the perceived urgency of the situation ensures that we continue to think inside the box, to carry on doing things just the way we have *without* allowing space and time for thinking about how we might solve the ills of the multilateral trading system. As Alan Winters put it during that moment wherein scholars and pundits alike presumed the Uruguay round was on the edge of a precipice:

> [for] many commentators the era of liberal and multilateral international trade is in the melting pot, if not actually doomed. To them the Uruguay Round . . . represents the last chance to re-assert the virtues of multilateralism which, if unsuccessful, will herald a descent into restricted and bilateral or plurilateral trading arrangements. (Winters, 1990: 1288)

What is important here is that the rationale for the GATT was consciously constructed for a particular purpose. That rationale brought with it a constructed history that has since become a core part of commonsense knowledge about the GATT. As such, it represents only a partial, subjective and problematic account of both the GATT and the logic upon which it is based. The language deployed, particularly relating to the dangers of not pursuing multilateral trade, is nevertheless sufficiently compelling and reasonably close to the historical reality to have become *the* story. This, in turn, has assisted in generating and maintaining a consensus around both the GATT/WTO as an institution and the kind of liberalization pursued therein. In the absence of a credible alternative, it has focused attention on fettling, but nevertheless persisting with, the existing system rather than fundamentally overhauling its core practices and attendant principles.

These metaphors and their related ways of talking do not of course constitute the sum of the ways we have chosen to express our subjective and politically instrumental view about trade.

Susan Schwab, for instance, has asked us to imagine that the act of trying to conclude a multilateral trade round is one akin to 'pole-vaulting' (2011: 104). Elsewhere, Bhagwati has suggested that seeing the round as a 'hanging' might just be enough to focus minds and get the negotiations going again. He has also claimed that the *Financial Times* was 'cluster-bombing' the negotiations, likened proclamations of the 'death' of Doha to Mark Twain's premature obituary, and suggested that the 'Doha Lite deal being attempted in Bali, is like a decaf . . . coffee' (Bhagwati, 2011; CUTS, 2013). And Duncan Green (2011) has encouraged us to see the WTO as sliding into a 'zombie' state of irrelevance.

What talking in these ways does is to limit discussion. In so doing it excludes from the realm of debate other solutions; an acceptance that periods of reflection may indeed be useful and essential components of trade rounds, and an acknowledgement that at particular times it might not be possible – politically or otherwise – to close a deal. Moreover, talking about trade in this way also encourages respondents to engage with the chosen metaphor, twisting it to fit their point of view. The consequence, however, is that in so doing they become bound up in a language, and a realm of political possibility, from which they cannot escape. Hence, counterclaims of the need for 'intensive treatment', 'incisive surgery', 'palliative care' and the like to save the round fail to get us beyond Doha as life-and-death struggle. In short, they force us to think about solving the ills of Doha in too high-pressured a fashion, crowding out time for measured contemplation of the problem, goal and solution.

The use of terminal medical metaphors, as with those requests for us to think of trade rounds as akin to material things that need to be kept in motion, are unhelpful. They create a pressure to act with speed that is not always helpful. They are also discursive tools that belie ideological dispositions and claims about how trade ought to be organized. They encourage us to take a leap of faith. And they belie empirical evidence which suggests that despite the round's problems and the onset of the recession since the negotiations ground to a halt in 2008, there has been no significant 'backsliding' or new protectionism (Siles-Brügge, 2013: 2).

Targeting recalcitrants

It is also worth noting that much of the leverage that the crisis discourse is designed to realize is directed at developing countries. The run-up to the 2005 Hong Kong ministerial conference provides a good example of this, though similar examples can be found in the run-up to many of the WTO's ministerial conferences. It was precisely because developing countries were seen to be the principal spoilers of any deal that might be struck that the crisis discourse began to be tailored towards what the consequences might be for them were the round to fail.

Former World Bank President Paul Wolfowitz, for instance, argued that:

> The stakes are too high – not just for the poor, but also for the global economy – to let the trade talks conclude without real progress. The Doha Round presents an opportunity to rewrite the rules of an unfair trading system that holds back the potential of the poorest people . . . [I]f Doha fails it's the world's poor . . . who will suffer most. (Wolfowitz, 2005)

Likewise, in a speech to the United Nations Conference on Trade and Development (UNCTAD), former WTO DG Pascal Lamy warned that:

> Hong Kong is not just another checkpoint in the negotiations. It is our best chance to move this Round to a successful conclusion . . . If we fail, we would all have lost a unique opportunity to rebalance the world trading system to the interests of developing countries. (Lamy, 2005)

As one developing country delegate put it at the time,

> we [developing countries] feel continually on the back foot. Because we were seen to get our way in Cancún, we were being

steadily forced to agree to positions [in the run-up to Hong Kong] we didn't feel comfortable with and sometimes didn't even understand, yet we were being warned of what might happen [to the multilateral trading system] if we didn't [agree to move forward].[16]

These sentiments were echoed by Dipak Patel, former Zambian Minister of Commerce, Trade and Industry and Chair of the Least Developed Countries Group, when he put it that 'the LDC group feels the most pressure to conform. We do not want to be blamed for another collapse or for any harm that might be done to the multilateral trading system'.[17] Barbadian Minister of Foreign Affairs and Foreign Trade and Vice-Chair of the Hong Kong ministerial conference Antoinette Miller noted that the pressure to reach an agreement, even though the expectations had been rolled back, had been motivated as much by the necessity of maintaining forward momentum and avoiding a repeat of Cancún as it had been about the substance of the agreement itself.[18] Likewise, a senior figure in the South African delegation to the WTO stated that despite the rolling back of expectations in the run-up to the meeting 'the pressure was . . . incredible. Many of the developing countries felt that if a deal wasn't reached they'd be primarily to blame'.[19]

The point here is that the intensification of the crisis discourse in the run-up to the Hong Kong ministerial conference played a role in ensuring that despite continuing tensions over the shape and direction of the negotiations an agreement was reached. Significantly, this intensification involved key core trade public intellectuals as well as those only peripherally connected with trade. This, in turn, helped shape the way delegations approached the negotiations and influenced the reframing of the negotiations in such a manner that preventing their potential collapse was perceived to be the overriding objective.

This strategy remains a key part of the ratcheting up of the discourse that occurs in the run-up to ministerial conferences.

As USTR Michael Froman, in his keynote address to the October 2013 WTO Public Forum put it 'if Bali shows that the WTO is not a viable forum for negotiations, bilateral and plurilaterals will likely be the only avenue for trade negotiations . . . [and] small countries and poor countries would feel the loss the most' (WTO, 2013b).

The WTO the unfortunate

One final construction warrants our attention in the twists and turns of contemporary trade discourse – the presentation of the WTO as a rather unfortunate institution. What is important about this construction is that is behoves us to accept that the organization is far from perfect, that it was the product of compromise, and in some way we should pity it and nonetheless get on with what passes for liberalization under its auspices. This is the invocation of an organization born out of opportunism and happenstance, imbued – not unsurprisingly – with certain 'birth defects' (Jackson, 2000: 15) rendered slightly less than fit for purpose and unfairly caught up in the crosshairs of trade politics.

Yet, as we know from Chapter 1, closer examination of the historical record suggests that rather than a slightly hapless body we find an institution quite well suited to the task at hand, whose performance has actually been quite strong in terms of the objectives that it was set up to achieve and whose development has been consistently focused on the task ahead (see Wilkinson, 2011; Ismail, 2011). Moreover, far from being the slightly unfortunate institution caught in the crossfire of great-power trade politics, the WTO is a more instrumental body that has been more effective and dynamic than is commonly understood and whose basic form and function have changed little since its creation.

These commonsense narratives do of course play an important role in the politics of global trade governance, even though – and often because – they obscure much of what is going on. Equally, while there is much to the governance of global trade that is underplayed or unappreciated, as we have seen this is largely a tale of institutional evolution that has enabled dramatically different trade gains to be accrued by participating states. For the leading industrial states, successive trade rounds have delivered important market openings and enabled restrictions to remain in key areas. We also know that for developing countries as a group – inasmuch as generalizations like this are useful – 8 rounds of negotiations have resulted in significantly fewer economic opportunities and have actually helped accentuate, rather than attenuate, global gaps between those who have and those who do not. Yet, we continue to paint a picture of an organization that struggles to function thereby obscuring the asymmetric gains that this mechanism of liberalizing trade has produced. There is, in short, little to pity.

Conclusion

We should bear in mind that even the best of the earliest accounts of the genesis of multilateral trade offers a partisan narrative. This is perhaps inevitable as the telling of history is, of course, always subjective (Carr, 2001: 2). It is nevertheless worth noting that like most histories, the lenses that are deployed tend to be tinted in ways that reflect dominant ideas and interests. The standard history of the GATT is no different. Most accounts focus on the GATT as seen from the viewpoint of Washington, London and Brussels. Few explore the role developing countries have played, leaving aside much of the industry and energy many exerted in the GATT's negotiation and evolution. Instead, developing countries tend to be portrayed as either determinedly negotiating relief from various commitments, focused on the pursuit of industrialization through import substitution and/or free riding on the commitments made by their industrial counterparts, or else as 'quiet bystanders' lacking the expertise or political representation to participate fully, or attempting to redress biases in the institution's design. Either way, the presentation of their participation in this way is used to encourage developing countries to reciprocate for (often inappropriate) concessions received and to become 'paid up' members of the trading system.

It is also worth reiterating that the received history of the multilateral trading system – and the metaphors and ways of talking that have come to perpetuate its commonsense logic – has come to dominate, in part, because alternative ideas either do not exist or else they have been discredited, and in part because of the path-dependent way of thinking that this history and its underlying set of assumptions encourages. The consensus that has emerged around the current global economic model has, in turn, solidified further the logic presented by the narrative of the GATT and WTO and has, inevitably, focused attention on the pursuit of minor adjustments for the sake of efficacy rather than fundamental reform. While it may well be widely acknowledged that the WTO is not working well – particularly for its least-developed members – the dominance of this model continues to underpin perceptions of the WTO as the only, or perhaps better still, the least ineffective game in town.

The stories that we commonly encounter about the GATT/WTO are not neutral, objective accounts; rather they are subjective accounts that encase a core political purpose – the advancement of a set of national trade interests – in a commonsense story about the value of free trade. One of the many problems of course is that these accounts tend to be incongruous with one another. The GATT was established as a mercantilist instrument in which some areas of commercial activity were to be liberalized while restrictions were to remain in others. This continues to be the case with the WTO. Equally, the necessity of keeping liberalization in perpetual motion is at odds with the record of trade politics wherein some areas have been opened up, others have remained protected, while others still have seen more protection emerge as other barriers to trade (particularly non-tariff barriers) have been imposed. And all of this has occurred in the absence of a slide into war. This of course does not mean that we should discard these stories as wholly meaningless. It means that we should acknowledge them for what they are: particularist views of how the world ought to be governed.

The task ahead is thus to reconstruct an alternative trade narrative that better captures the history of the multilateral trading system, that uses the past as a motivation for change, that has at its core a concern for the interests of all, and which enables broader debate to occur in a less ideologically constrained fashion – a task to which the next part of this book turns. Yet, it is precisely because the narratives that inform the multilateral trading system have proven to be so malleable, and accommodated challenges and accounted for changes through time that they have continued to exude an appearance of relevance.

Part II

Solutions

CHAPTER FOUR

Thinking differently?

As the preceding chapters show, there is much that is wrong with the way liberalization has been pursued under the GATT/WTO, the means by which trade openings are negotiated, and the way we think and talk about trade. We are not honest with ourselves if we imagine we can 'level the playing field' in an adversarial system designed precisely to use every advantage available to produce inequitable outcomes, which always was and continues to be so intimately connected to the pursuit of a set of developed-world interests, and wherein debate is clouded by ideological positions presented as commonsense facts and linguistic turns of phrase.

Yet, stating that the multilateral trading system requires reform is far from revelatory. Proposals for reform of the multilateral trading system have been on the agenda since the first GATT negotiations were conducted. Nonetheless, much time and effort continues to be dedicated to the issue. Calls for reform fill the pages of broadsheet newspapers, weekly periodicals, internet forums, NGO bulletins and myriad other outlets in the run-up to, during and following a WTO ministerial conference; and developing new and innovative proposals has become a staple activity in-between. WTO reform has also occupied the time of many a consultative group, commission, committee, practitioner, policymaker and academic alike both during moments of heightened interest in the organization and during 'quieter' periods (see Deere-Birkbeck, 2009; and Hoekman, 2011 for good overviews).

The result of this intensive industry has been a lively, if not altogether fruitful debate. Two aspects of the debate about WTO reform are nonetheless noteworthy. First, few proposals find purchase beyond the constituencies to which they speak and for which they are produced. Of the large number of non-governmental organization (NGO) and civil society organization (CSO) proposals only those produced by the largest, most connected and/or most politically acceptable receive much external attention (see, for instance, Oxfam GB, 2000; CUTS, 2010; Meléndez-Ortiz, Bellman and Mendoza, 2012). Second, despite the volume of proposals produced, there is remarkably little that separates them substantively beyond a chasm between those who broadly support the idea of a world trade organization and trade liberalization as a vehicle for growth and development, and those who challenge the WTO's very existence or else seek its circumscription (Bello, 1999; Peet, 2009). And given that the latter are dismissed out of hand by mainstream commentators and those who have the capacity to affect organizational change in the short to medium term, the arena of thinking on this issue is extraordinarily small.

As a consequence, we seldom think critically about the purpose, function and future of the WTO. More often than not we start with the system as it is and offer finite measures to address aspects of its operation. We do not raise more foundational concerns, or question the fundamental tenets of the system. One consequence is that we settle for 'inside the box' thinking offering proposals that ultimately perpetuate a problematic system and which obscure the capacity of the WTO to serve as a machinery for delivering equitable outcomes for all, particularly the poorest and most vulnerable. Even some of what we imagine are the more 'radical' ideas about reforming the WTO take the existing system as it is and seek merely to alter particular aspects. Stiglitz and Charlton's (2013) ideas about enshrining a 'right to trade' and a 'right to development' in the WTO's Dispute Settlement Mechanism (DSM) and the creation of a Global trade Facility are good examples of innovative but nonetheless inside-the-box thinking.

The result of continuing to think inside the box is to eschew fundamental reform. Yet, in the absence of a fundamental overhaul that goes beyond the kind of reform that dominates the most frequently touted proposals, future trade negotiations are unlikely to produce outcomes that are markedly different from those of previous rounds or that are likely to result from the DDA. The viciousness of the circle does not end there. When we are confronted with another asymmetrical bargain, as Doha is likely to produce (and as the Bali package foreshadows), we are likely to turn once again to fettling, but nevertheless preserving, the way the current system works rather than substantially changing or overhauling it (as we have and are doing with the turn towards 'plurilaterals' in the Doha round). And because we have always tended towards piecemeal reform – and it appears as if we will continue to do so – it is likely that trade negotiations will continue to result in an exchange of concessions that will be of relatively greater value to the economically more significant trading nations than their developing counterparts. Of course, this does not rule out reforms of value being implemented in the near future. It does mean, however, that in the absence of a fundamental departure from existing ways of governing trade, few prospects exist for the realization of development gains for all or for a new era in multilateral trade.

It is not always obvious what incremental reform looks like or what its consequences are, however. Yet, distinguishing between 'system maintaining' and 'system transforming' reform is an essential endeavour if we are to change fundamentally the manner in which trade is governed (and to do so in a way that promotes development-for-all). We need to be aware of the longer-term consequences of the reform options we put our weight behind. We need to recognize that there is a spectrum of what is 'deliverable' and what is less likely to be achieved. We also need to recognize that most of the options that are deliverable are likely to lie on the system-preserving – rather than system-transforming – end of the spectrum. And it is precisely because of our frustration with, and the hitherto pragmatist approach to reform of the WTO that we have – consciously or otherwise – concentrated the bulk of our efforts on perpetuating the status quo end of the spectrum.

This chapter begins the task of thinking about a fundamental transformation of what the WTO is and does by considering the most prominent proposals for the organization's reform. Its aim is to distinguish system-maintaining reform from that which is genuinely system transforming – the subject of the two following chapters. Its purpose is to draw attention to the status quo-preserving consequences of the most commonly touted and significant reform initiatives and proposals. Its argument is that in almost all cases, ideas for reforming the WTO seek merely to alter one component of the system or else tweak very modest aspects of existing operational machineries. They seldom attempt wholesale reform, particularly of the sort that addresses the system's fundamental tenets. In discussing each of the major proposals in turn, my purpose is to set the foundations for a re-orientation of the way we think about the WTO in the chapters that follow.

Responses to WTO malaise

In many ways the Doha round has and is unfolding as a hybrid of the Uruguay and Tokyo rounds. Like the Uruguay round the blockages seem bridgeable only once a new track of negotiations opens up exploring the functioning of the multilateral trading system (what was the Functioning of the GATT System – FOGS – during the Uruguay round and which is being proposed as the Functioning of the WTO – FOWTO – now and/or what has been unlocked by the agreement of the Bali package);[20] and like the Tokyo round, entrenched positions in thorny areas seem navigable only by switching to plurilateral negotiations among the major players in issue-specific areas. Some of these trends have been 'spotted' by commentators who have then developed them into plausible reform proposals which, in turn, have been disseminated and something of a consensus built up around them. Other proposals have been developed in ways that speak to aspects of either the need to streamline negotiations (the plurilateral route) or improve an aspect of the functioning of the WTO (the FOWTO route). Yet, a third but much less obvious movement has occurred – reforms that have *already* taken place and which have been evolving 'under the radar' – and which have sought to address both the way negotiations are conducted and the functioning of the system. In all, five distinct 'responses' are discernible, all of which have brought with them particular reform proposals:

(i)   the 'under the radar' response;
(ii) the call to plurilaterals;
(iii) the limited-scope response;
(iv) the coherence response; and
(v)   the changing economic geography response;

Response 1 – under the radar

With the exception of the director general and one or two other high-profile figures (normally deputy directors general – DDGs – who in any case are co-opted ambassadors from member states rather than secretariat employees), the secretariat rarely features in debates about the future of the organization. It has, however, been deeply affected by the deadlock in the Doha negotiations; it has formulated a strategy designed to play its part in securing the survival of the institution; and aspects of this strategy have *already* been put into place. Yet, this has gone almost unremarked upon.

We have missed this at our peril. Although the secretariat's strategy appears to be largely the consequence of growing institutional maturity (in terms of 'naturally' encouraging the growth of particular activities) it represents some of the most radical institutional consolidation in the history of the multilateral trading system. This is not a system-changing radicalism, however. Rather, the secretariat's response is notable precisely because it is status quo consolidating. In formulating a policy to ensure the organization's continued relevance the secretariat has sought to demonstrate what it is that the WTO does rather than embark on a process of fundamental reform.

This response is perhaps inevitable when a body of employees are working hard to ensure the survival of the institution in which they are employed; but it can create the kind of resilience that militates against change. Yet, while it is the case that the secretariat's response most definitely lies on the system-maintaining end of the spectrum, the kind of resilience it has shown may well prove useful in pursuing a more transformative strategy later on – a point to which the next chapter returns.

Three aspects of secretariat response require note:

(i)   the arrangement of negotiations and the good functioning of the organization;
(ii) the organization of ministerial conferences and of WTO-sponsored public meetings; and
(iii) the establishment of ancillary functions and activities that are designed to establish an independent credibility by distancing the organization from what goes on in negotiations.

The role of the secretariat – and the DG in particular – in the arrangement of negotiations is a long-noted feature of trade rounds. In order to facilitate agreement, the DG and the secretariat have often advised on the appointment of chairs of the various negotiating committees and the agenda and content of discussions, and offered the services of key personnel to assist in various activities. Moreover, members of the secretariat and the DG have chaired these committees and their influence on the outcomes has been obvious as a result – during the Uruguay round, for instance, GATT DG Arthur Dunkel put forward a text designed to navigate between entrenched positions and which, with some minor amendments (notably in agriculture), formed the basis of the legal documents that led to the establishment of the WTO (see Thomas, Singh, Kanitkar, Ahmed and Johnson, 1994) – and the secretariat has acted as a 'clearing house' for information on positions reached and proposals tabled by key members and negotiating groups.[21] Much like the model on which it is based – an international version of a nominally 'apolitical' civil service – the capacity to exercise influence in these ways is at first glance limited but not necessarily peripheral, as the Dunkel text amply illustrates. Indeed, at key moments during the Doha round the secretariat's input into the arrangement of negotiations has been instrumental in getting negotiations restarted (no matter how temporarily). In other instances, the secretariat – and the DG in particular – has gone out of its way to be seen *not* to be influencing the outcome of negotiations by resisting the temptation to author (or authorize) a negotiating text. This was a key feature, for instance, of DG Azevêdo's organization of the Bali ministerial conference (see Wilkinson, Hannah and Scott, 2014). Even in these instances, however, it has been the secretariat (principally the DG) that has organized and facilitated discussions.

It is of course unremarkable that the secretariat would operate in this way. The intention would always be for an administrative body to act in a fashion that supports the work of an organization helping with the realization of key goals. What is of note is that whenever the secretariat operates in this way it merely patches up and adds to the longevity of a form of global trade governance that requires a fundamental overhaul. It is, in other words, a self-reinforcing – that is, system-maintaining – strategy.

The second aspect of secretariat response relates to the way it has addressed the growing politicization of the trade agenda. This response has evolved over time and has focused primarily on the external face of the institution though two distinct phases are discernible. In the first, the secretariat sought to keep public interest in the organization and its work at arm's length, with the responsibility for civil society engagement in WTO and related affairs firmly placed with member states. This was manifest not only in the production of a set of guidelines for relations with NGOs (see Wilkinson, 2005a for an extended discussion), but also in the creation of a 'public forum' (initially established as the Public Symposium) wherein civil society representatives could engage with the organization *outside* the confines of ministerial conferences. It was no coincidence that the first public forum was held in July 2001 in the wake of the inflammatory 1999 Seattle ministerial conference and in the run-up to the November 2001 Doha ministerial meeting (at which the DDA was launched). This public engagement strategy was complemented with the rolling out of an 'education' programme which comprised the production of a series of information guides to the work of the WTO, as well as a huge investment in, and up-scaling of, the organization's website to correct what the secretariat saw as a number of errors in public perceptions about the institution and its work. The most notorious of these was the '10 common misunderstandings about the WTO' which has subsequently morphed into '10 things the WTO can do'.[22]

The extent of public ill-feeling at the global trade agenda caught the secretariat very much on the back foot and the production of early information documents like '10 common misunderstandings . . .' reflected a knee-jerk and defensive response on the organization's part as did the attempt to deflect criticism from itself and direct civil society attention towards member states as the 'appropriate' venue for raising issues of concern. This was, however, to change. If phase one of the secretariat's response was defensive and 'educational' (in that it sought to combat criticism by disseminating its own subjective ideas about what it is that the WTO is and does), phase two has been principally about political neutralization. This change in policy has been most evident during ministerial conferences as well as during public forums but it has also been manifest in a shift in the language of publically available documents and the way the institution now presents itself virtually (a shift to which the move from '10 common misunderstandings . . .' to '10 things the WTO can do' amply illustrates).

In seeking to diffuse some of the political tension around meetings the secretariat has had some success. With regard to ministerial conferences the secretariat has been able to meet the obligation of hosting these meetings while at the same time divorcing them from the 'heat' of the negotiations and the ire of civil society. This was the case at both the 2009 and 2011 Geneva ministerial conferences as well as – less expectedly so – at the 2013 Bali meeting (which was sparsely attended by representatives of civil society). As James Scott and I (2010) noted with regard to the 2009 Geneva conference:

> In sharp contrast to its previous ministerial gatherings, the World Trade Organization's 7th Ministerial Conference in Geneva (30th November to 2nd December 2009) proved to be something of a success. This was perhaps not surprising. The meeting was actively engineered from the outset to be a 'non-event', an institutional stock-taking exercise, and a routine gathering rather than an ambitious negotiating session attracting large scale demonstrations and political grandstanding among the delegates. As WTO Director-General Pascal Lamy (2009) put it in the closing session of the Conference 'I tried to surprise you all with a no surprise user-friendly ministerial meeting, something you haven't had for a while!'. In that Lamy succeeded.

We continued,

> While the patter of the conference contained nothing [else] that surprised the 3,000 gathered delegates representing 153 members and 56 observers, the fact that nothing was at stake and that

Table 4.1. WTO public forums and symposia

2013 – Expanding trade through innovation and the digital economy
2012 – Is multilateralism in crisis?
2011 – Seeking answers to global-trade challenges
2010 – The forces shaping world trade
2009 – Global problems, global solutions: towards better global governance
2008 – Trading into the future
2007 – How the WTO can help harness globalization?
2006 –What WTO for the XXIst century?
2005 – WTO after 10 years: global problems and multilateral solutions
2004 – Multilateralism at a crossroads
2003 – Challenges ahead on the road to Cancún
2002 – The Doha development agenda and beyond
2001 – Symposium on issues confronting the world trading system

there were few precise objectives, ensured that a 'successful' outcome was inevitable (in that the meeting did not break down or result in yet more inertia being injected into the increasingly moribund Doha round of trade negotiations). Yet, the meeting's only real 'success' was that it was hosted in such a way that enabled some of the political heat to be taken out of WTO Ministerial Conferences moving the institution back to a more technocratic pace. This was precisely because, as Faizel Ismail, Head of the South African Delegation, put it, 'there is zero going on',[23] a lack of industry (particularly with regard to the Doha round) which Alan Beattie likened to 'the rough equivalent of holding the 1919 Versailles conference without talking about the war'. (Beattie, 2009)

This strategy of neutralization has also been evident in WTO public forums (Table 4.1). A distinct shift has occurred in the nature of the forums, moving from venues in which civil society could be educated about the WTO and a place for public engagement with the organization, to a politically neutral venue populated less by 'the public' and more by representatives of business and the legal profession taking advantage of the networking opportunities such gatherings now afford. Such is the extent to which these events have been neutralized that attendance at the October 2013 gathering was a fraction of the 1,500 the secretariat claims normally attend. Almost none of the major civil society players chose to put forward panel proposals for the sessions available. The second of the two plenary sessions was led by a particle physicist (Rolf-Dieter Heuer, Director General of the Conseil Européen pour la Recherche Nucléaire) who by his own admission had little to say that was about trade (and, it should be noted, whose presentation had little connection with the rest of the session). Very few of the panels comprised anyone with a core role in the WTO or the Doha negotiations. And the topic of debate – 'expanding trade through digital innovation' – was hardly the best choice just two months prior to the crucial Bali ministerial conference (or indeed the most cutting-edge topic being as it was at least a decade behind the curve). So successful has the secretariat been at nullifying the value of the public forum that ambassadors, delegates and civil society representatives alike openly expressed their dissatisfaction and their intention not to attend in the future.

The third aspect of the secretariat's response has been to establish ancillary functions and activities designed to lend the organization credibility, independently of what happens in the negotiations. This has comprised, among other things, the significant up-scaling of the institution's data collection and analytical capacity, a joint initiative with the OECD to measure 'value-added in trade', and a significant increase in the number of working papers produced. The secretariat has also made extensive use of video and podcast technology, YouTube, and Twitter – though the latter was not in evidence at the 2013 public forum (frankly because there was very little to 'tweet' about). It has established a 'chairs programme' – identifying and appointing university professors with the title of 'WTO Chair' – ostensibly aimed at supporting the developing world in its trade policy strategies and designed to build lasting relationships with the institutions involved by encouraging members to engage in outreach and communication activities and establish links with think tanks, but which actually has only appointed scholars uncritically disposed to the status quo. And in 2011 the WTO launched its Youth Ambassador Programme (YAP) designed to increase awareness of trade issues among younger people, to encourage their participation in public discussions on this theme, and to introduce new perspectives to debates – albeit targeted at disseminating the 'right' kind of knowledge rather than facilitating genuine debate.

It is hard not to be cynical about the secretariat's three-pronged response. Whether it is the way it helps arrange negotiations, the neutralization of political contestation during ministerial conferences and other public meetings, or the selection of a winner from the YAP, the emphasis is on promoting the 'right' kind of knowledge about the WTO rather than stimulating critical thinking or engagement. And while this might be an entirely understandable strategy for a secretariat feeling the heavy weather of a stalled Doha round, the consequence is to preserve a system that delivers asymmetrical gains and which eschews genuine movement forward. That said, the siege mentality the last decade and a half have lent the secretariat has the potential to be a positive force in a more fundamental programme of reform (to which we return in Chapter 6).

Response 2 – the call to plurilaterals[24]

A second response that illustrates precisely what should not be done to solve the ills of the Doha round or the precarious situation in which the WTO finds itself, but which has been long (and now increasingly loudly) touted as a way forward, is to change the shape of negotiations away from a single undertaking – a negotiating commitment to all members signing off on all aspects of a bargain – toward allowing subsets of countries to negotiate 'plurilateral' agreements (see Saner, 2012; Huang, 2009; Oyane, 2001). The logic here is that progress in the round – and indeed future rounds – can only be secured if a few likeminded countries with a sufficient share of world trade are permitted to get together and negotiate issue-specific agreements that open up trade (see Draper and Dube, 2013 for an extended discussion).

As we have seen, this approach to trade is far from new. What is new is the gusto with which the idea is being advanced and the way it is being presented as a panacea for moving the round forward. Indeed, such is the energy behind the drive to plurilaterals that in some quarters it is being suggested that, should the broader membership agree to allow this form of mini-lateralism to play a major role, it might be one way that development gains could be smuggled back onto the agenda (though it is hard to see how this could realistically be the case unless various development-focused plurilateral negotiations were launched in conjunction with those intended to expand economic activity in cutting-edge sectors). We should not be so quick to forget what past experience teaches us about plurilaterals.

One of the most interesting aspects of the emerging debate is the volte face that has occurred in the way that some in the trade community have come to view plurilaterals. Prior to the December 2011 conclusion of the Government Procurement Agreement (GPA) and the moves by the Real Good Friends of Services to negotiate an International Services Agreement, plurilateralism was widely held up by serving officials of member delegations (but not commentators ,some of whom were former negotiators) as undesirable. The role of plurilaterals in shaping the Tokyo round (1973–9) accords and in distributing trade gains to a small and select group of countries in an otherwise multilateral setting led many to criticize this à la carte form of negotiating, preferring instead broad-based single undertakings. The selective fashion in which plurilaterals were used to forge agreement during negotiations, and which bound only a small number of signatories with an interest in the area (i.e. the industrial states), was vociferously opposed by developing countries during the Tokyo round. During the July 1978 meeting of the Trade Negotiations Committee (TNC), for instance, the developing countries lodged a collective complaint about the exclusionary and isolating nature of small-group and plurilateral negotiations arguing that 'major decisions should be taken at meetings in which all countries, including developing countries, [are] able to participate' (cited in McRae and Thomas, 1983: 78).

In the current renaissance, plurilateralism is being defined as any form of mini-lateralism that covers agreements in specific sectors and/or a subset of members. Thus, bilateral and regional agreements (such as NAFTA) are all now being recast in some quarters as plurilaterals – a much broader definition than previously seen. In turn, plurilaterals are being depicted as building blocks of the multilateral system – much in the same way we are encouraged to think about regional trade agreements. Sitting squarely behind the changing discourse on plurilaterals is a concern with the direction of US trade policy. The TPP, TTIP, and official assertions that the United States will satisfy its trade objectives by any means, have combined to put the proverbial cat among the pigeons.

Our collective memories tend to be short, as much of the recent debate has seemingly forgotten that the turn towards plurilateralism was and is a strategy that has been used frequently when a blockage in a multilateral trade negotiation has arisen; and the eventual outcomes of these turns have invariably been asymmetrical. Indeed, as Chapter 1 showed, the very multilateral trade system that we have is itself the result of a plurilateral turn. There are numerous other occasions wherein the turn to plurilateralism has either prevailed or generated a pressure to move forward multilaterally. Yet, when the idea of a mini-lateral solution to a multilateral problem is put on the table we forget this and act with such relief that plurilateralism is entertained as if it was a new idea. Even in the context of the DDA the idea of a mini-lateral solution has been circulating for several years. The difference has often been the moniker – with variable geometry and club of clubs being two of the most familiar (see, for instance, Lawrence, 2006; Sutherland Report, 2004; Cornford, 2004) – though they are at root plurilateral solutions.

The historical record makes it clear that small, vulnerable and least-developed countries should be concerned with the current shift towards plurilateralism. Throughout the post-war era, many of the smallest least able developing countries were excluded from such agreements. This happened for two principal reasons: (i) because of their already noted lack of negotiating capacity; and (ii) because plurilaterals were almost always driven by the major powers and the subjects chosen for negotiation inevitably those in which they have greatest economic interest. Recent plurilaterals – such as the Information Technology Agreement and GPA – bear this out. It is worth reminding ourselves that the poorest countries have few information technology exports and therefore little interest in securing freer trade therein; and entering the GPA would open up government contracts to foreign competition while at the same time prohibiting the award of those contracts solely to domestic suppliers as part of a national development strategy.

Yet, such is the desire to get the DDA moving that these highly exclusionary approaches are being considered. Topics currently mooted for plurilateral treatment include intellectual property, services, technical standards, product safety and e-commerce, all of which are of central concern to the advanced industrial states but few of which offer benefits to the least developed. By contrast, attempts to construct an 'early harvest' in the areas of commercial interest to the least developed – such as duty-free quota-free market access, agriculture and trade in low-technology manufactures – have achieved only limited success and even then they have required significant trade-offs to be agreed (such as in trade facilitation), as the 2013 Bali package attests (see Wilkinson, Hannah and Scott, 2014).

Advocates of the plurilateral approach argue that it offers the opportunity for willing members to move forward, leaving others to join later. However, there are inherent problems with signing agreements which are written without one's participation. As we saw in Chapters 1 and 2, throughout the negotiations on any trade measure the states involved seek to ensure that their particular interests are reflected within the final document, thereby establishing first-mover advantages (Keohane, 2002: 253). Those not invited to sit at the table cannot do this. Moreover, they frequently find that if they wish to join an agreement at a later date it is rarely constructed in a way that addresses their particular concerns (as it would have been if they had been a first mover) and often requires that they pay a higher price – in terms of concessions given away – for late entry.

Four further points are noteworthy. First, history shows us that plurilateral agreements are also frequently rather limited in the benefits they bring to the industrial states. For example, two of the Uruguay Round's plurilaterals – on Dairy Products and Bovine Meat – were terminated just two years after the WTO's creation because they failed to result in the negotiation of meaningful disciplines. Second, trade issues that are too divisive are often impossible to reach agreement on in any forum, plurilateral or otherwise. Any substantive plurilateral agreement that sought to include, for instance, the USA, EU, Japan, China, India and Brazil, would likely result in failure as it is these countries that have struggled to find agreement within the DDA's small group meetings – hence the re-emergence of plurilateral fora (such as TPP and TTIP) as leveraging devices designed to force the hand of competitors in the wider Doha negotiations. Third, the historical record suggests that real gains for industrial countries lie in a multilateral solution that enables them not only to gain preferences in other developed-country markets but which also enables them to exploit the future market potential of large developing countries, which is why the industrial countries were so keen on a single undertaking in the Uruguay round as they had also been during the previous Tokyo round until its realization became impracticable. Fourth, when taken in the long run it seems that it is the Uruguay round single undertaking (problematic as it was) that is the historical anomaly. Most of the previous GATT agreements were plurilateral in one way or another – either because they were designed as limited agreements reflecting agreements forged in areas of possibility (as was the case with the Tokyo round) or else they were agreements that did not bind the contracting parties as a whole (as was the case with the other rounds). It is precisely because gains were not maximized in the previous rounds that a multilateral solution was, and is preferred.

Thus, it remains the case that plurilaterals offer little – short or long term – for least-developed, developing and industrial countries alike. Their return to the agenda is one motivated by an expediency designed to salvage something from the round and a hope that their negotiation might act as a lever to a broader multilateral deal. As such, the pursuit of plurilateralism is not a strategy that will address the fundamental problems of the multilateral trading system. Rather it will continue to ensure that global trade is governed by the outcome of competitive negotiations among states of dramatically different size and shape wherein the will and whim of a small collection of the most powerful states predominate. The only hope is that further recourse to plurilateralism will reinforce the need for a root-and-branch rethink of the multilateral trading system – though in the medium term it is most likely that a plurilateral turn will reignite interest in a single undertaking eschewing in the process anything other than system-preserving reform.

Response 3 – the 'limited scope' response
A third response to the ills of the Doha round and the quagmire in which the organization finds itself is for commentators to

emphasize what the WTO is *not*. The purpose of this exercise is to present the institution as so limited in scope that it cannot possibly hope to deal with all of the issues with which it is confronted or in which secretariat officials and critics alike do not wish to see it engage (see Wallach and Woodall, 2004; Monbiot, 2003). For others, it is about identifying and dealing with the limits of the WTO's scope in a technical fashion (see Jansen, 2011). On occasion, the call to limit firmly the scope of the WTO is made in tandem with a stated need for some kind of high-level panel or conference on WTO/UN agency coherence (see, for instance, Sampson, 2004). For Bhagwati, this exercise is essential to halt 'the steady encroachment by rich-country lobbies to impose their unrelated agendas on trade agreements' (2005: 28; also 2001). Elsewhere, it is designed to put an end to debate that the WTO is, or could be, the basis of world government (see, for instance, Moore, 2003: 11, 235; McGinnis and Movsesian 2004: 2).

Proclamations limiting the scope of the WTO emerged almost as the organization began operations. Suggestions that its remit could be expanded to incorporate a host of issues led to a number of contrary pronouncements. Some, like Andrew Guzman (2002), sought to explore the WTO's utility as a basis for a World Economic Organization (WEO), an idea also developed by Marco Bronckers (2001). Others examined how WTO-style 'trade-related' agreements (such as the TRIPs and TRIMs) could be extended to other areas, such as labour standards (see Hughes and Wilkinson, 1998). These suggestions were, in turn, countered by claims that an extension of WTO activities might be used as a pretext for discriminatory action and had no place in a trade institution (see Wilkinson, 1999). Former WTO DG Mike Moore's infamous quip that 'labour is a false debate' (WTO, 1999b) was one of many designed to preserve the organization's trade-only remit.

This policing of the WTO's boundaries has, however, taken a rather odd turn of late. Over the course of the Doha round certain commentators – and the organization itself[25] – have been at pains to point out that the WTO is *not* a development organization (see, for instance, Lamy, 2006; Mavroidis, 2011: 376). Instead, they claim that the WTO's purpose is to facilitate an expansion in the volume of value of trade. This, in turn, will encourage growth and development leaving the organization to worry about trade and trade alone. The paradox here is of course that if more trade equals more growth, which in turn leads to more development, then surely any organization that is concerned with facilitating more trade must *by definition* be a development organization? And if this is the case, then we ought to recognize that it is and act accordingly. This logic is of course recognized, but the conclusion is drawn that the WTO is and should remain a *trade* agency (see, for example, Mavroidis, 2011).

It is this paradox, more than anything else, that gets to the heart of the question: what is the point of the WTO? If we ask ourselves that question and come up with an answer which says that we want a system that consistently delivers unbalanced trade deals favouring the richer industrial states over their poorer, less able developing counterparts, then let us fiddle round the edges and leave the institution largely as it is. If we come up with an answer that says the WTO should generate trade-led growth for all (something that we all ought to be able to agree on), then we need to redesign it as such, getting rid of competitive negotiating as a mechanism for delivering 'gains' and accept that in facilitating trade-led growth for all it will inevitably become a development institution (and we should accept that it is one). This point is taken up again in Chapter 6 when we discuss how a series of progressive reforms could be put in place that move the organization in a fundamentally different direction.

Response 4 – the coherence approach
Like the response of the secretariat and of calls for a new round of plurilaterals, the limited-scope response is a strategy designed

to preserve the status quo. In demarcating the WTO's zone of operations, the organization is encased in a manner that restricts any capacity to change. A related suggestion – but in many ways the obverse of the limited-scope response – is to more coherently connect the WTO into a system of global economic governance working on its 'fit' with other intergovernmental organizations. In some ways, these calls for greater coherence also serve to reinforce the status quo; in others they present opportunities for more progressive – and in the longer term – fundamental reform.

If the purpose of limiting the scope of the WTO is to underline the need only to focus on one institutional machinery that if left to function will as a second-order consequence sort out the world's problems, the coherence agenda is driven by a desire to connect the WTO up more organically with a wider constellation of institutions in the formation of global public policy. Behind this desire lies a hope that institutional change will be affected in bringing the WTO more firmly into a global institutional family and co-ordinating policies therein. Some point out that moving the WTO in this direction would merely complete a form of institutional nestedness – as I have argued elsewhere (Wilkinson, 2002) – that was intended to be a feature of the post-Second World War system and which was half-heartedly done at the WTO's creation (via a set of limited declarations nominally connecting the WTO up with the work of the IMF, World Bank, WIPO and others). Others explore instances of coherence and incoherence in the WTO's mandate with a view to improving the fit between it and other global economic institutions in the pursuit of better global public policy (Bernstein and Hannah, 2012).

While these attempts are laudable, their utility rests in a hope that some of the more negative aspects of contemporary trade governance can be addressed passively (rather than actively) by bringing the WTO more firmly into an inter-institutional context. Past experience does not, however, suggest that such a strategy would necessarily work – as anyone with any experience

of the remit policing and institutional rivalry among UN institutions will know only too well. A deeper problem, however, is
that it would leave the WTO largely intact. Any reform would be
excruciatingly slow and would not address the core problem of
bargaining among unequals and the production of trade governance by asymmetrical outcomes as a result. Moreover, the overall
effect would not be to make global governance more effective;
rather it would be to install and legitimize in a wider complex a
problematic machinery of governance.

At one level, then, while calls for greater coherence may leave
the WTO more or less intact – and would certainly fail to address
the problem of bargaining among unequals – at another level
building coherence in key areas (development, environment,
health and so on) is a necessary prerequisite for a fundamentally reformed system of global trade governance that focuses
on development-for-all. Moreover, if managed in the right way,
a coherence agenda may not leave the WTO or any other of the
global institutions (UN Development System, Bretton Woods
and the like) intact. In this way, coherence can be thought of as
a means, not an end. It is not just about sorting out the messy
boundaries that lie between the zones of operation of various
intergovernmental organizations (which is the concern of much
of the coherence literature); it is about fitting those institutions
together into a coherent whole that has a distinct social purpose.
In this version of the coherence agenda, better global economic
governance is a necessity for a fundamentally reformed WTO precisely because the root problem of incoherence is manifest in the
way macroeconomic and trade institutions make and operationalize policies that are contradictory and are disconnected from
core development, social and environmental goals and priorities.

As Steven Bernstein and Erin Hannah (2012) point out
coherence is poorly understood, it lacks a common and robust
conceptualization, and it often comes without a coherent
and cogent programme of action. One consequence is that

conversations around coherence tend to focus on relations between institutions eschewing important normative and policy considerations. For Bernstein and Hannah, coherence is better defined as the systematic promotion of mutually reinforcing policies across three dimensions (environmental, social and economic). In this formulation, a coherence agenda necessarily has institutional, ideational, normative and policy components. And if engineered correctly (that is, in contrast to what currently exists) such an agenda can be fundamentally transformative. These are important and fruitful foundations upon which we can build – to which we return in Chapter 6.

Response 5 – the changing economic geography approach

Comparably well meaning are assertions that more pluralism is required when it comes to the way decisions are made among the major trading powers in negotiations. Many have argued that the global economic and trading landscape has changed since the GATT and WTO were created and core decision-making in the institution needs to be reformed to reflect this (see, for instance, Singh, 2008; Calbin, 2008). Motivating many of those who put forward suggestions such as these are concerns with improving the democratic credentials of core decision-making in the WTO as well as enhancing its legitimacy. And in many ways these calls reflect what has already happened. The old quad (United States, European Union, Japan and Canada) has been replaced by the G4 (United States, European Union, India and China) and some-times by the 'Five Interested Parties (the G4 plus Australia). It nonetheless remains the case – as it did when the quad was in the ascendency – that decision-making requires agreement first and foremost between the United States and the European Union. It is only then that a second 'inner' circle is brought into the fray.

Yet, whether WTO decision-making is formalized around the new trading powers, altered on the hoof to reflect whatever changes may occur in the constitution of global economic power, or expanded to include more members, none of these reforms suffices. The problem is that they would still leave intact a system of governance that distinguishes between the advantaged (the core decision-makers) and the disadvantaged (those who are not involved and whose participation is ensured to the extent that they are offered a degree of involvement on a take it or leave it basis). This is akin to reforming the UN Security Council by expanding the number of permanent members (with or without veto power and/ or a nuclear deterrent) to reflect changes in global-power configurations. Only a small number of countries would still have the power to make and enforce decisions, leaving the vast majority excluded and their interests not represented. So, while reforming WTO decision-making to include new members (in a formalized fashion or otherwise) may satisfy a desire to reflect more accurately changed global power relationships, it would leave intact a system of governance that privileges the interests of the few over the many.

Moreover, in addition to merely changing who occupies chairs at the top table, reforming the WTO in this way would not alter the resentment that most would feel at the continuation of small-group domination of a global trade body or the system-preserving nature of reforms such as these. No one any longer argues that it is democratic to allow the richest to have more votes than the poorest in domestic political systems or that votes should be distributed on the basis of wealth. Yet these arguments still circulate in ideas about, as well as the practice of international relations (witness the distribution of voting in the World Bank and arguments to recalibrate it). What is needed instead is an elected council that comprises representatives from states at all levels and from all regions appointed on a fixed-term non-renewable basis without a distinction – de facto or otherwise – between permanent and non-permanent members. Yet such a system could only hope to work if the WTO's machinery of governance were also altered fundamentally (to which we return in the next chapter).

Conclusion

If the GATT/WTO has primarily served as a means of managing trade in the interests of a small subset of countries and we have confused what it does as free or freer trade – as this book argues – then we need a radical rethink not only of the organization but also of the way we think about the organization. It is also fair to say that this rethink needs not to be fashioned in the form of responses that either reinforce what it is that the WTO currently does (as the responses above illustrate) or which merely tinkers at the margins, but which thinks much more broadly about the purpose and value of the organization.

Yet it is understandable – given the difficulty of reforming any aspect of the WTO – that most commentators should err on the side of caution and advocate proposals that, while being well meaning, are narrow and lacking in ambition. Calls to carve out 'policy space' for developing countries (Gallagher and Wise, 2009) are important in lending poorer countries greater agency in the formulation of domestic industrial strategies and mirrors what it is that developed countries are able to do. In the absence of a comprehensive and coherent strategy in which they are embedded, however, they do and will not fundamentally change the way trade is governed. The same is true with calls to enhance the functioning of the dispute settlement process, add various consultative committees, make further improvements to the institution's transparency and legitimacy credentials, develop hard and fast rules governing negotiations, do away with/make modifications to the principle of consensus, adjust rule-making and management processes, and bolster and/or refashion Special and Differential Treatment and enhance proposals for Aid for Trade (see, for instance, Cottier, 2007; Tijmes-Lhl, 2009; Steger, 2009; Warwick Commission, 2007), among others. As stand-alone proposals they add seasoning to the pot of debates about WTO reform, but none of them in isolation addresses the fundamental problem with the system – that is, the way trade is governed through bargains struck between unequals. The more difficult task is to think about a programme of reform that does.

The problem, then, is that many of the reform responses outlined above merely patch up an already problematic system, addressing small anomalies in institutional design, but failing to alter fundamentally the kind of outcomes that are produced. What is needed instead is a much more wide-ranging discussion and set of proposals about the WTO as an institution, its purpose, form and function. The problem of course is that because beginning this conversation – let alone developing something radically different from what we have today – would challenge the status quo, we are likely to continue to concentrate on piecemeal reform, ensuring that trade negotiations will continue to result in an exchange of concessions that will be of relatively greater value to the economically more significant trading nations than their developing counterparts. Yet part of the problem with debate about the WTO and its reform is that because major reform is unlikely commentators have tended to focus on what might be deliverable, thus engaging in a pitched battle over very little and certainly not a lot that matters. What we need to do, and what the next chapter does, is think about a reformed world trade organization as if we were given carte blanche before returning to the more pragmatic task of working out how we get there.

CHAPTER FIVE

Trade for all

When we think about the WTO we think of a rather technical institution concerned simply with the rules and regulations
governing trade at the global level. We tend not to think of an
institution that has, or should have, a broader social purpose. Part
of the reason for this is precisely because – as we saw in Chapters
3 and 4 – the organization has sought to recapture an older technocratic image of itself, one that *does* stand apart and slightly
aloof from everyday life and which simply purports to serve the
member states to which it is responsible in a politically neutral
and expeditious manner. Part of the reason also lies in the way we
think of and talk about the organization. And part of the reason is
because the WTO – either the secretariat or its members – does
not think of itself as directly serving a social good. Certainly, it
(the secretariat and the member states) and those commercial
interests that it is supposed to serve conceive of the organization's work as bound up in nurturing an activity – trade – from
which will flow social outcomes. Yet these are outcomes that are
seen as one step removed from the core work of the institution.
As former DG Pascal Lamy put it in his statement of what it is
that he imagines the WTO does:

> The WTO's founding and guiding principles remain the pur-
> suit of open borders, the guarantee of the most-favoured-nation
> principle and non-discriminatory treatment by and among
> members, and a commitment to transparency in the conduct of
> its activities. The opening of national markets to international
> trade, with justifiable exceptions or with adequate flexibilities,

will encourage and contribute to sustainable development, raise people's welfare, reduce poverty, and foster peace and stability. At the same time, such market opening must be accompanied by sound domestic and international policies that contribute to economic growth and development according to each member's needs and aspirations . . .

[To this end the] WTO provides a forum for negotiating agreements aimed at reducing obstacles to international trade and ensuring a level playing field for all, thus contributing to economic growth and development. The WTO also provides a legal and institutional framework for the implementation and monitoring of these agreements, as well as for settling disputes arising from their interpretation and application.[26]

Three aspects of this statement are important for our purposes. First, for Lamy it is the opening of national markets to international trade that is the primary purpose of the WTO, from which it is assumed development and welfare-enhancing, poverty-reducing, and peace-and-stability-generating effects will flow. Thus the social purposes of the WTO are secondary to the primary purpose of opening markets. This is not a case of mere semantics. If the primary purpose of the WTO was to produce development, welfare-enhancing, poverty-reduction, and peace and stability effects, and the machinery for realizing those effects is an opening of national markets, then it would be changes in the former against which the performance of the organization would be measured, rather than whether trade barrier reductions resulted in markets being opened further. When presented the other way round, as it currently is, the WTO's performance is measured on its capacity to facilitate market openings – and even then only some markets (see Wilkinson, 2011) – and not whether it has welfare-enhancing and other effects (which may or may not result). The corollary of this is that positive changes in social indicators lie somewhere in a haze over the horizon and are eschewed for a focus merely on market openings.

Second, in the pursuit of opening up national markets to international trade, a claim is made that the organization's purpose is also to provide a level playing field through the provision of a negotiating forum aimed at reducing obstacles to international trade. Yet, what we have seen consistently throughout this book – but particularly in Chapter 2 – is that bargaining among unequals in an institutional context that favours the industrial countries is very *unlikely* to level the playing field. Moreover, attempts to overcome the effects of power asymmetries and skewed rules – principally manifest in the formation of coalitions – have done little other than generate deadlock and stalemate.

Third, for Lamy (and many others) the WTO's role is intended to be purely technocratic – that is, the governance of the world-trading system by those best able to operationalize the legal and institutional instruments for implementing and monitoring WTO agreements as well as for settling disputes arising from their interpretation and application. It is not intended that the organization itself actively engages in socially beneficial activity; merely that it serves the 'will' of its member states, with which it is deemed resides the ultimate responsibility for agreeing upon such activity.

Not only does this account of what the WTO is and what it does stand in marked contrast to most of the major (particularly UN) intergovernmental organizations, it is an unsustainable and undesirable state of affairs. While it might be the case that international institutions have, since their creation, predominantly served dominant state and business interests some have also been at the forefront of generating socially progressive ideas (see Murphy, 1994; 2006). This is as true for the ILO, WHO and the Food and Agriculture Organization (FAO) as it is for the UN Development Programme (UNDP) and the World Bank (a claim that will surprise many that are critical of this institution). While it might also be the case that these institutions have frequently at been at odds and indeed loggerheads with one another over their competing visions of the world (sometimes productively so), they have at least been engaged in trying to make the world a better place through the pursuit of specific mandates (Murphy, 1999: Thérien, 2005; Jolly, Emmerij and Weiss, 2009). We may rightly dislike some of the policy prescriptions of these organizations (see, for instance, Wade, 2001; Weaver, 2010; Harrison, 2004) but they can at least be said to having been engaged in the construction and implementation of policy that has a social purpose (even if at times the way they approach that purpose appears to be rather inappropriate).

Yet, the WTO belongs to a class of global institutions (in which we might also include the IMF) whose mandate is purely technocratic, which claims social outcomes only as second-order consequences of the fine management of the global economy, but which – in their very functioning – nonetheless put forward a vision of how the world is and should be, without being held up to, and accountable for, a specific mandate. This is a problematic state of affairs. Not only does the WTO exercise considerable power in the construction of a global commercial framework it also – along with other global institutions – has an effect on shaping the economic opportunities available to member states. It is unthinkable that we would now create a global institution of such significance which did not have a progressive social agenda as its core motivation.

It was not always this way in the governance of global trade and both the GATT and WTO retain vestiges of broader social mandates from a bygone era. The ITO had a very specific social purpose that spoke to the needs of the post-war era. It was intended as the fulcrum organization in a triumvirate of global institutions whose primary purpose was the reconstruction of global trade as the vehicle for pursuing full employment (the barometer against which the performance of the organization could be judged – see Gardner, 1956). Its partner organizations in this endeavour were to be the IMF and World Bank (or as it was then, the International Bank for Reconstruction and Development, IBRD).

The Havana Charter – the ITO's foundation document – is replete with references to the social needs of the era and the Charter was itself the outcome of a UN conference on trade *and* employment. Its founding objects committed the organization to:

- assure a large and steadily growing volume of real income and effective demand, to increase the production, consumption and exchange of goods, and thus to contribute to a balanced and expanding world economy;
- foster and assist industrial and general economic development, particularly of those countries which are still in the early stages of industrial development, and to encourage the international flow of capital for productive investment;
- further the enjoyment by all countries, on equal terms, of access to the markets, products and productive facilities which are needed for their economic prosperity and development;
- promote on a reciprocal and mutually advantageous basis the reduction of tariffs and other barriers to trade and the elimination of discriminatory treatment in international commerce;
- enable countries, by increasing the opportunities for their trade and economic development, to abstain from measures which would disrupt world commerce, reduce productive employment or retard economic progress;
- facilitate through the promotion of mutual understanding, consultation and co-operation the solution of problems relating to international trade in the fields of employment, economic development, commercial policy, business practices and commodity policy. (UNCTE, 1948: 14)

It matters not that the Charter was itself a document borne out of a compromise between genuine worries about social cohesion in the wake of post-war demobilization and the memory of the inter-war depression, progressive social aspirations, tense politicking and hard-nosed commercial interests, or that the US decision not to submit the Charter to Congress for ratification relegated the ITO to the annals of economic history. Nor does it matter that some of the language of social purpose contained in the Havana Charter and which was carried over into the GATT was more cut-and-paste than principled focus. What matters is that the ITO stands as an example of a form of global trade governance that had the achievement of social goals as its primary purpose and which was connected up to a strong normative agenda with an attendant policy programme to which the fine management of international legal mechanisms was subordinate.

This is neither a naive nor a rose-tinted view. The ITO was far from an ideal institution. Its legal framework was replete with provisions that were stacked in favour of special interests; and the Charter was cumbersome and largely unworkable. The point is simple. We need a form of trade governance that is engaged in the fine management of global commerce. But we need one that serves a broader social purpose as its primary function and not one that sees an increase in the volume and value of trade as an end in itself then crosses its fingers and hopes that all else will be well.

My purpose in this chapter is to sketch out what such a trade organization could and should look like. In the next chapter I set out a roadmap for how this might be achieved. Here, my purpose is to get us to look up and see the bigger picture, to expand the arena of what we imagine is politically possible, and to start from a different place when thinking about reform of the WTO.

As I have said above, we need a world trade organization; yet we need a mechanism for governing global trade in a way that is beneficial to us all, one that is concerned with not only what we can trade (goods and services) and how we go about organizing that trade (the rules and regulations), but also the outcomes produced by the way we organize trade. Constructing such an organization is neither beyond our imagination nor capability.

We all broadly agree on what should, and should not be traded. Moreover, we worry about the manner in which we govern trade (that is, the way it is organized). It follows, then, that we should also worry about the consequences – that is, the outcomes – of the way we manage trade. We would not trade goods that could be used in the construction and development of nuclear technology, for instance, if we did not first give thought to how that trade ought to be regulated or what the consequences of trading in those goods might be – however imperfectly we have done it. We would no longer design an international legal framework that actively disadvantaged the few over the many. So why should it be different for the totality of global trade when we know full well that the impact of the way that we currently organize trade has been an unequal distribution of economic opportunity that advantages those who are already advantaged and disadvantages those who can ill afford it? It is with this in mind that the rest of the chapter unfolds.

The next section explores precisely what the purpose of a world trade organization should and could be. Here the chapter focuses on connecting up the work of global trade governance with broader social aspirations. The chapter then discusses how the organization – its legal framework and ways of operating – can be refashioned to meet those objectives. This in turn lays the foundations for Chapter 6 which explores how we could get from where we are to where we should be going.

Making the WTO globally relevant

It is difficult to imagine that an organization that has been so caught up in political crosshairs and whose primary function has been largely deadlocked for more than half a decade would survive if there were not a broad consensus that it is an institution of importance, if not relevance. Equally, it is difficult to imagine that we would choose to persist with a form of governance that is broadly considered to be of importance but which has been found to be malfunctioning without a programme of reform. Yet, the various crises in which the WTO has been plunged, and the stalemate and malfunctioning that has ensued, have clearly not generated the degree of institutional precariousness that is perhaps required to focus minds on the need for a radical overhaul to secure its long-term future. And there appears to be little hope that such a moment may transpire anytime soon.

Despite the relief that the Bali package may bring, its agreement may actually serve to prolong rather than attenuate this state of affairs. It may be, as I have argued elsewhere (Wilkinson, 2006a), that crisis has actually played an important role in moving the institution forward and, in so doing, reinforcing existing ways of operating – hence it is just what we expect. It may in fact be – hyperbolic and empty declarations of the WTO's 'death' notwithstanding (see Wilkinson, 2012) – that the response of the secretariat to deadlock in the Doha round has shored up the rest of what it is that the organization does. It may also be because the lion's share of political responses, pundit commentary and academic literature on WTO reform has tended toward incremental fine-tuning and not more far-reaching and radical solutions. What if, however, the organization's very existence were actually imperilled? Would the response of the secretariat or of those concerned with the organization's reform be the same? The chances are that our responses would be quite different, that we would be forced to think more innovatively and radically about how to make the organization more relevant, and that this would generate a robust and coherent strategy.

We do not have to look far for an example of precisely the kind of organizational precariousness that has generated a realizable response and coherent strategy which is worth considering momentarily. The institution is the ILO – though we might also have considered the IMF or World Bank, both of which underwent fundamental changes in their operational mandates and driving objectives at key moments in their history – and its experience is one from which we can learn a great deal but one that we have not yet (openly at least) considered.

Despite the WTO inhabiting the old ILO building on the shores of Lake Geneva (albeit the building has now been significantly extended), relations between the two organizations have always been a little 'frosty'. Not only do the two institutions regard themselves as occupying different places on the global ideological spectrum, their entanglement in the trade and labour standards debate of the late 1990s and early 2000s fostered a conscious effort to put distance between them despite a commitment to continue 'existing collaboration' (which was essentially very little – see Haworth, Hughes and Wilkinson, 2005). Yet, there is a lot that is instructive about the ILO's institutional development from which the WTO can learn.

Since its creation in 1919 the ILO has demonstrated a capacity for institutional resilience and innovation that has kept it relevant at times when the organization's very existence has been called into question (Hughes and Haworth, 2010: 5–19). Much of this resilience and innovation is attributable to the leadership of successive directors-general and the concerted efforts of a secretariat intent on ensuring the organization's relevance. A key component of this strategy has been to undergo a process of periodic rejuvenation at moments when the very existence of the organization has been threatened. Certainly, these moments have not rendered the ILO wholly unproblematic. They have, nonetheless, enabled the ILO to survive the transition from League of Nations to United Nations at a point in time when that transition was far from certain. It was able to stave off the threat posed by the creation of the United Nations Industrial Development Organization (UNIDO) in the 1960s (Jacobson, 1969: 84; Cox, 1973: 110). It has ensured that that the ILO remains relevant in an era when the old sources of its strength and support (largely organized labour) have fallen back. And the organization has kept pace with fundamental changes in the nature of work and the new and varied forms of precariousness that afflict workers worldwide. As Robert O'Brien puts it (2013: 152): 'the ILO has been able to survive for the past 90+ years due to strategic leadership, an ability to reposition itself to address the challenges of its times and the work of highly technical staff providing policy relevant advice'.

A Philadelphia moment

How exactly did the ILO do this? The history of securing the ILO's continued relevance is told in full elsewhere (Hughes, 1999; Alcock, 1971). For our purposes, one particular part of that story is illustrative. Crudely put, in the shadow of an uncertain future the ILO began attempting to secure a place for itself within the nascent post-Second World War institutional order. Initially, this did not prove to be an easy task. The ILO was not officially invited to the Dumbarton Oaks (on the structure of the United Nations Organization) and Bretton Woods (on the reconstruction of the global economy) conferences. Nor was it mentioned in the Dumbarton Oaks proposals. It was only invited to attend the San Francisco Conference (establishing the UN) after considerable lobbying; and, as a consequence, it was not mentioned in the UN Charter (Johnston, 1970: 78–9). Nevertheless, on 14 December 1946 the ILO made the transition from League of Nations to UN, securing a place within the latter's framework as a specialized agency (Phelan, 1946: 281–4). How?

Three aspects of the ILO's strategy are instructive. First, ILO DG Edward Phelan convened a conference (which took place 20 April to 12 May 1944 in Philadelphia) designed to reaffirm the organization's credentials and underline its centrality to the post-Second World War reconstruction effort. Second, the outcome of the conference – the Declaration of Philadelphia[27] – refined and updated the ILO's aims and objectives reorienting the work of the organization around the core normative human rights agenda of the about-to-be established United Nations. Third, as a necessary corollary, Phelan paved the way for the ILO to become a UN family institution. In combination these and other factors 'saved' the institution, ensuring its continued relevance and placing its work squarely within the wider aims of the United Nations system (Hughes and Haworth, 2010: 13). As Edward Phelan put it in his 1946 address to the UN General Assembly:

> when restating its aims and methods in the Declaration of Philadelphia, [the ILO] recognised that its aims could not be achieved nor its methods prove effective, if it worked in isolation, and so it pledged in advance its co-operation with such other agencies as might have had committed to them the responsibility of international action in the framework of a world organization. (Phelan, 1946: 282)

The point here is that after a quarter of a century in operation, the ILO restated and refreshed its core purposes, enabling the organization to recapture a focus and update its objectives in light of changed global circumstances and a new normative and ideational climate. This repositioning saw the work of the organization placed firmly within the context of the wider achievement of the peace and security, and human rights agendas of the UN establishing the direction and purpose of the ILO as one of achieving wider social goals rather than the realization of employment regulations in the workplace as an end in itself. Moreover, in securing the organization's place as a UN body this strategy embedded the ILO firmly within a wider global public policy arena.

This strategy is pertinent to the WTO precisely because although the organization has quasi-formal relations with other organizations – largely the Fund and the Bank but also WIPO – it remains independent of the UN system. It illustrates how a restatement of the organization's purposes can give renewed focus and orientation correcting the flow of responsibility (that is, that the achievement of wider social goals as the priority to which the reduction of barriers to trade are merely a vehicle). And it shows how by embedding the institution within the broader UN complex in a way that speaks to the kind of progressive coherence agenda Bernstein and Hannah (2012) advocate would assist in that reorientation as well as the achievement of those wider social goals (rather than pitching the organization at odds with various UN institutions as is often the case). Simply put, the WTO needs a new socially progressive set of aims and objectives that connect it up with the agendas of other global bodies.

For Stephen Brooks and William Wohlforth (2009) there is reason enough to overhaul fundamentally our global institutions and reconsider the purposes for which they were designed. As they put it, the 'existing architecture is a relic of the preoccupations of power relationships of the middle of the last century – out of sync with today's world of rising powers and new challenges, from terrorism and nuclear proliferation to financial instability and global warming' (Brooks and Wohlforth, 2009: 49). For the ILO a quarter of a century was long enough to justify a period of serious and productive institutional introspection. As we have seen in the previous chapters this need is particularly acute in the WTO's case especially given that it has remained largely unchanged since the GATT was first negotiated in 1947.

What precisely would this mean for the WTO? A new declaration of aims and objectives ought to place the realization of trade-led development-for-all in an environmentally sustainable fashion at the forefront of the purposes of the multilateral trading system with particular emphasis on helping the least able; and the operation of any machinery for that purpose must not be judged on reductions in barriers to trade or estimated projections in the overall contribution that these reductions will make in the aggregate. Rather, the system ought to be judged on its capacity to generate welfare-enhancing opportunities for all (including enabling those most disadvantaged to make use of those advantages). And the new aims and objectives ought to be suitably ambitious. If the World Bank can have as its two primary goals 'an end to extreme poverty within a generation' and a 'boost to share prosperity' we really are talking about small beer when we consider what the WTO currently has as its driving objectives.[28]

Clearly, such a restatement and reorientation of aims and objectives cannot identify the WTO as the institution with sole responsibility for generating equitable global welfare gains; but it certainly does need to connect the organization more organically with its sister institutions; and it needs to do this in a way that improves the policymaking coherence among those bodies, as Bernstein and Hannah point out (2012). Here again, however, we cannot simply insert the WTO into the existing system, stir, and expect the problem to be fixed. What needs to happen simultaneously is a process of wholesale reflection on what it is that our global economic (and other) institutions do, how they do it, and what their purpose is. Too many of our global organizations have continued evolving in unreflective ways eschewing fundamental reform and making only incremental adjustments but not actually thoroughly revising what it is that they do (see Weaver, 2010; Momani, 2010; Weiss, 2009). Perhaps we ought to utilize the opportunity that the prolonged stasis in the WTO has created and contrive an ILO-esque Philadelphia moment for all global institutions, setting out a framework, strategy and roadmap that offers a coherent and compelling way forward.

Such a moment would by necessity bring the WTO into much closer collaboration with UN institutions than is currently the case. Indeed, the idea that greater coherence in global economic policymaking ought to take place, that it should deal with issues that have been hardy perennials of macroeconomic policy since before the GATT was created, or that the WTO should become a UN institution are not new – I make no special effort to advance the latter here but rather note it as a necessary corollary. What is important for our purposes is to:

(i)   show how a process of institutional reflection can be a catalyst for an organization that has not looked at what it is and what it does (but has merely got on and done it) since it was first created, that inherited its statement of purpose from an organization that was stillborn (the ITO), which was designed with different aims and objectives in mind, and which spoke to different interests;

(ii) point out how that reorientation should change the focus away from the removal of barriers to trade as an end in itself to one wherein the achievement of broader social goals is the organization's primary reason for being; and

(iii) underscore the necessity of doing this in tandem with a fresh look at what it is that all of our global institutions are doing for us.

It is important to emphasize that the necessity for a moment of reflection and for reorienting what it is that the institution does should not be a one-off. As we know, all too often institutions evolve in ways that are tightly constrained, moving forward only incrementally and unchangingly, making them quickly out of step with changed external circumstances. This is particularly so with the global institutions that we have, most of which have at some point been seen to be superfluous and which have, as a result, spent too long justifying their own existence and not long enough moving forward in doing what it is that they ought to. Hence, the point of an ILO-style Philadelphia moment is not just to correct the anomalous way that the WTO currently operates, but also to put in place a process by which reflection becomes a normal part of the institution's movement forward.

As an aside, it is worth pointing out that reorienting the WTO (and other global economic institutions) around core UN goals has the added benefit of bringing with it a measure of legitimacy. The strategic direction of the UN's development focus, for instance, is the outcome of a broad process of dialogue and engagement that brings together a vast range of actors. Frustrating as this process may at times be, it is not the consequence of a consensus borne of hard-nosed politicking or coercion, or the technocratic decisions of a board of directors or shareholders chosen for the size of their economic interests. And while they are not unproblematic, the processes by which the norm of poverty reduction was negotiated and became manifest in the Millennium Development Goals (see Wilkinson and Hulme, 2012), and the manner in which the post-2015 development regime has been crafted, do lend a direction from which our global economic institutions could and should benefit.

The WTO as a trade-led development-for-all organization

So what ought a restatement of the WTO's core purposes to do? Refreshing the WTO's aims and objectives has to segue into the necessity of reorienting it as a trade-led development-for-all organization. Here we need to think carefully about what we mean by 'development-for-all' and clearly distinguish this from the negative associations that have long infused, implicitly and explicitly, debates about 'development'. As we noted in Chapter 2, the construction of broad categories of states such as 'developed' and 'developing' is largely arbitrary and often means little beyond helping to leverage a particular kind of politics into a conversation. It is these conversations that infuse the kind of tensions that Weiss (2009; 2012a) complains about and that have rendered companion dichotomies and trichotomies – east/west, rich/poor, core/periphery, first/second/third world, developed/developing/least developed – equally problematic.

One of the many consequences of these catch-all terms is that they flatten out important distinctions between and among countries. They also hide the extent to which most states combine sectors that vary dramatically in terms of their own development. To suggest that India, Brazil, South Africa and China are strictly developing countries ignores the leading-edge sectors that each country comprises. Equally, their elevation up the international pecking order as 'rising' powers obscures the structural problems that each has as well as the large tracts of enduring poverty and destitution not to mention – with perhaps the exception of Brazil – growing inequalities. Equally problematic are the labels we assign to the 'developed' world. As many have pointed out, parts of the developed world harbour populations that inhabit conditions that are little different to their counterparts in the global South. This is as true of the lived experiences shared by the poor in urban centres like Los Angeles and Houston as it is of São Paulo and Guangzhou.

Most metrics and serious intellectual interrogations render these stratifications problematic (Payne, 2005: 6–11, 36–44) as do understandings of the extent to which global economic geography is changing (Dicken, 2011). This of course does not mean global di- and trichotomies cease to generate modes of politics and contestation which are often exacerbated by the iterative games that are played out in trade negotiations. What is required instead is a form of organizing trade that recognizes the multifaceted nature of global economy and of nation-states and to move away from a form of governance based on competitive negotiations as the machinery for realizing economic advantage to one that is more focused on fostering trade for all. Such a reorientation would ensure that the WTO is much more like a global version of a national department of trade and industry – an idea to which we return momentarily – and much less like a device designed to serve the interests of some and not others. And it offers us the conceptual volte face that we require to move the WTO beyond the state it is in.

An approach that recognizes the necessity of trade-led development-for-all moves away from states as the focus of global public policy toward people. We know well and understand the contradiction between states negotiating international legal frameworks and economic actors operating under their auspices.

A focus on trade-led development-for-all would correct our gaze. It would focus our attention on the problems of particular individuals, communities and industries and their capacity or not to engage in economic behaviour. And it is in targeting them, and their capacity to make the most of an enabling environment, that would be a more appropriate reorientation of a world trade organization.

The key here would be to identify areas wherein special assistance is required and to divert resources and attention accordingly. This of course does not mean that leading-edge sectors and new and novel forms of trade should be ignored. It simply means that in the development of an enabling environment for all – distinct from one that has evolved in a fashion that has actively harmed the trade opportunities of some – the poorest and least able receive special attention. These communities should not be identified because they are constituents of poor countries alone; we should realize that resources and knowledge also need to transfer to sectors in the developed and middle-income worlds, but they are most likely to attract the lion's share in the short to medium term.

A global department of trade and industry

If we understand that like any national economy, the world economy has areas that are highly advanced, others that are not, others still that languish or are in decline, or else they lie somewhere in between, and we marry this to an understanding that the goal of any global organization ought to be to provide welfare gains for all, then the task of a world trade organization ought to be to strategically intervene to help those areas of economic activity that require assistance, regulate against abuses (such as monopoly power), and develop strategic initiatives that assist in the further development of all sectors, among other things.

The typical response to suggestions like these is to state that we do not have a world government and that the creation of a competitive system is the consequence of bargaining among sovereign states (for instance, VanGrasstek, 2013: 3). This argument falls down on many counts, three of which are pertinent here. First, since the idea of a world organization was first touted and elements of it first put into place (initially under the League of Nations and then the United Nations) we have had a system of global regulation that governs global economic (and other) behaviour and which mimics the design of the governmental apparatus of a nation-state (see Mazower, 2012). In this way, the UN, its specialized agencies and programmes, and other world organizations that co-ordinate life on this planet represent, as Craig Murphy puts it, 'what world government we actually have' (Murphy, 1994: 1).

Second, many international organizations regularly transgress – and on occasion intentionally circumscribe – state sovereignty in their operations. While the retort to this observation is normally that these instances are often the result of a sovereign decision to join an organization (which is taken as the necessary consent for such activities taking place), this is not wholly accurate. As a range of authors have demonstrated, for most developing states (not to mention their developed counterparts) sovereignty is often more imagined than real (Jackson, 1993; Duffield, 2005); and membership of many international organizations and programmes was frequently presented to developing countries as a *fait accompli* rather than as something to be considered (we need think no further than the requirements of many an IMF and World Bank structural adjustment programme for ample example). Moreover, a sovereign decision to agree to one thing does not presuppose that future agreements can or should be made without further consultation and, on occasion, plebiscite.

Third, the WTO is unique among global institutions in the enactment of a competitive and adversarial system as the means by which governance is exercised. Most others, though exuding elements of political contestation, do not for their everyday operation rely upon competition between members – this is as true for international environmental institutions as it is for the World Bank and IMF, the WHO, ILO and UNCTAD. This is not the way to operate a system of governance in an enlightened fashion. We have long since made the move away from grand global systems based on disadvantaging some for the benefit of others (as colonialism did); it is about time we eradicated the last vestiges of disadvantage.

The point is that global institutions are in some way designed to provide a global public good – irrespective of whether they also help cement wider arrangements of political power and advance the interests of the powerful therein. As public goods providers they have a responsibility to ensure equitable access to those goods, certain restrictions notwithstanding (a condition of restricting access to opportunities for trade-led growth as a global public good would not, for instance, be because a country is poor and inconsequential in global trade as is currently the case). We should take this commitment seriously, and press our global institutions to provide these goods in ways that are as fulsome as possible. We all know that the health of a national economy is affected by the underperformance of its weakest parts – we need look no further than Malcolm Gladwell's (2006) account of 'Million-Dollar Murray' for a popular illustration. The same is true of the global economy.

Refashioned in this way, a world trade organization ought to move away from adversarial negotiations as the mechanism of distributing economic opportunity to a form of governance that incentivizes and facilitates trade-led growth (an area in which the World Bank actually has more expertise than the WTO currently constituted). Thus the primary functions of the WTO should be to:

(i)   develop strategic plans and strategies for assistance that speak to and help realize wider socially progressive global goals;

(ii)   facilitate the transfer of knowledge about global trade in a way that is genuinely equitable and which speaks to the specific economic circumstances of recipients; and

(iii) establish a development fund designed to nurture trade-generating activities in hard-to-realize places.

Other desiderata could be to guard against monopolistic and anti-competitive behaviour. Crucially, the system would not work on the basis of *states* as the primary focus of attention but rather geographic areas and specific agents within, between and across states. Thus, the 'rust belt' in the United States and the de-industrialized parts of South Wales and northeast England would be eligible for trade assistance from a refashioned world trade organization as would subsistence farmers in Burkina Faso or shack-dweller co-operatives in Mumbai. Clearly, need would determine the direction in which assistance flows, as well as the kind of assistance that was offered (finance for trade in one area, knowledge transfer and legal expertise in another and so on) – though it remains the case that the lion's share of attention ought to be focused on the least developed.

Meaningful knowledge transfer

Another arcane aspect of the way global public policy is currently constituted is that there is no one co-ordinating centre for the transfer of knowledge. What exists instead is a profusion of actors that each offer and engage in the transfer of knowledge (and not always altogether usefully either). These range from official national development agencies and multilateral organizations and programmes to non-state sources (both for, and not-for profit). For many developing countries it is not always clear how these programmes can be accessed or how to navigate the special interests that underpin them. All too often these programmes are superficial and lack local contextualization and sensitivity. And there are reasons why economic actors in leading-edge sectors

do not want to transfer commercial knowledge and information
(which relate primarily to the negative impact that it might have
on their competitiveness).

The problems of knowledge transfer are well known and I do
not intend to rehearse them here. My point is simply to raise the
issue as one that ought to be a core feature of what it is that the
WTO does (in a much grander way than it currently does). The
kind of knowledge that would be transferred ought not to be tied
up with the secretariat's current strategy to secure its relevance
by recasting what it does – and preserving how things currently
operate – however, but rather with the sort of information that
speaks to a refreshed global trade institution along the lines set
out above. That said, the step change in the organization's capacity in data and knowledge production does provide a foundation
upon which a move in this direction could be made. Moreover, it
would naturally bring the WTO into a closer working relationship
with existing development institutions as well as with UNCTAD
(a relationship to which we return momentarily).

Real aid for trade

To be really effective as a machinery for promoting trade-led
development-for-all we need to put some substance behind, as
well as shift in a different direction, the current aid-for-trade
agenda. While the move to highlight the importance and necessity of aid-for-trade has been one of the very few positive outcomes
so far of the Doha round, the problems are legion and well noted,
two of which concern us here: (i) all too often what is presented
as aid-for-trade is repackaged development assistance; and (ii)
there is no overarching machinery monitoring or co-ordinating
its distribution.

There is much value in considering establishing a fund administered by the WTO designed specifically to offer trade assistance.
Not only would this add to the WTO's remit in a way that would
elevate it beyond a mere forum for contentious and adversarial

encounters, it would have a number of benefits, three of which are worth noting now. First, in assigning funding to a specific pool, the capacity of member states to count aid-for-trade twice or indeed several times in their overall development assistance budget would be mitigated. Second, the capacity of member states to tie this aid to specific interests and projects would be mitigated as it would be given through a multilateral agency. Third, there are extraordinary transaction costs that are incurred in the aggregate by a number of states all giving development assistance as well as economies of scale that are unrealized. Not only are the distributional aspects of their bureaucratic machineries replicated in each individual instance, the research and policy development aspects of their operations are also repeated. By combining funding in one pool, only one specific aid-for-trade machinery needs to be created drawing on only one research and development apparatus. Clearly this would have to be designed so that the fund was accountable and transparent, not to mention targeted at areas of need in a way that produces results (rather than giving for the sake of being seen to give). Nonetheless, it makes sense to leverage aid-for-trade funds out of the hands of member states into a multilateral pool administered by the WTO and appropriately constructed.

Merging competencies

If the replication of functions across a range of assistance providers is problematic, so too is replication of functions among the various global institutions that purport to have a role in trade. The time for two separate trade institutions in the form of the WTO and UNCTAD has long since past. While it was politically expedient for both North and South to have their own trade bodies, in a post-Cold War era – particularly one wherein more progressive social values need to rise to the top of the global agenda – the replication of activities in the two institutions is no longer sustainable. We cannot hope to work together in making the world a better place if we continue with two organizations working for different constituencies often in competition with one another and in an occasionally hostile manner.

Yet, it is not only merging the work of UNCTAD and the WTO that makes sense (and benefiting from the economies of scale that could result therefrom). Bringing into a large and more able institution the competencies of the ITC (an existing instance of co-operation between the WTO and UNCTAD) and others (perhaps UNIDO, the World Customs Organization, WCO, and WIPO to name but three) would also produce a more focused and fit-for-purpose institution. This coming together could be done in a federal fashion – perhaps via concordat – under the auspices of the UN Economic and Social Council (ECOSOC). It could be realized in one grand organization. Or it could be done in a variety of ways in between. The point is not that trying to fuse the organizations as they are currently constituted ought to be the focus of our attentions (the political tensions such an exercise would generate would be insurmountable) but rather that task repetition and institutional competition render our global institutions inert irrelevant in the eyes of casual observers, and serve poorly those constituencies that need them most. So, rather than present a blueprint for how this coming together could be achieved here, my purpose is to set out the case for the necessity of a single world trade organization.

System management

It is not just a horizontal bringing together of the various pieces of the existing trade architecture that could be pursued under the auspices of a single world trade organization. A more fundamentally reconstituted organization could act as a machinery for bringing a greater degree of coherence to the myriad bilateral and regional trade agreements that currently exist (one that goes far beyond the simple information gathering role of the WTO's Integrated Trade Intelligence Portal).[29] The idea here would be monitoring all trade agreements to determine their coherence – legally, substantively and outcome-wise – with a commonly agreed-upon set of global trade objectives.

This is a sizeable but a desirable task. Nowhere is there a formal, coherent and legitimate system of surveying and indeed governing bilateral and regional agreements or assessing their consistency with the multilateral trading system. The monitoring of member states' trade measures in the TPRM or the bringing of derogations to the attention of members via a dispute settlement case are too *ad hoc* to constitute sufficiently robust and consistent procedures. The point here is not to intervene in some way in the ongoing and rather circular trade-creating/trade-diverting debate. The point would be to provide a monitoring mechanism that lends coherence and transparency to the system, that requires members to ensure that *all* their sub-multilateral trading agreements (including those in place with non-members) are not only consistent with WTO law but that they are also consistent with a new focus on development-for-all and that they generate outcomes congruous with that, and other, objectives. This would add weight to a new global trade agenda and mitigate the pursuit of narrow and partisan interests in fora wherein safeguards against the abuse of power are fewer in number.

Pursuing greater vertical coherence in addition to bringing together the intergovernmental components of the global trade architecture ought to be considered a vital aspect of a fundamentally reformed system. Without it members would continue with the nominal requirement that all of their trading agreements are consistent with WTO rules but would in practice continue to allow derogations to exist and not be compelled to adopt demanding degrees of consistency. The effects of not bringing coherence to the system horizontally *and* vertically would be to render a transformed WTO at best impotent and at worst null and void. And the pursuit of a new multilateral trade agenda would have no chance of succeeding if at the bilateral and regional level it was still very much business as usual.

Governing global trade governance

It is impossible and highly undesirable for a new, grander, more socially orientated global trade order to be established and managed if the architecture for managing the system itself is not democratic, legitimate, transparent and representative. To ensure that appropriate checks and balances are in operation, such a system would require at least two distinct bodies – a wholly reconstituted (and fundamentally different) governing council and some form of stakeholder assembly. The purpose of two bodies would be to hold the system to account. Decision-making authority would reside with the governing council. This could be made up with, say, fifteen representatives from member states elected by particular constituencies. Representatives could neither be elected nor make first-order decisions without the agreement of the constituencies they represented. Ideally these constituencies would not be demarcated in accordance with existing ideas of representation relating to share of world trade, levels of development, geographical proximity and so on. Rather, each constituency would comprise a representative sample of each of these groups to ensure that a member of the council could not be elected as a representative of, say, developed countries, or for that matter Europe, North America, or agricultural producers. The fifteen constituencies – a reasonable number each representing a little over one-tenth of the membership – would have to adhere to a common set of procedures designed to ensure that one set of interests is not able to prevail. These procedures would include a requirement that council members be elected to non-renewable terms of five years, no country could have a representative elected for two consecutive terms or three terms in six, and the process by which the election takes place must be open and transparent.

The stakeholder assembly would act to ensure that the governing council was operating in a manner consistent with the goals of the organization. Ideally, it would comprise state and non-state stakeholders. Such a constitution may include representatives, in equal number, of members that do not also have a member currently elected to the governing council, business groups, and consumers/civil society interests. Again, strict guidelines would have to be drawn up to ensure that each member of the stakeholder assembly was selected in an open and fair way and which militated against a particular set of interests prevailing. Preferably, the terms of tenure of council and assembly members would be different, with elected members of the assembly serving non-renewable periods of three years against the governing council's five.

Cutting-edge innovation, development and knowledge transfer

The task of fundamentally reforming the WTO should not be seen as one wherein the institution is whittled away, but rather one in which it is substantively and fundamentally reoriented and simultaneously strengthened. As we saw in the last chapter, one way the secretariat has responded to repeated crises in the Doha round is to scale up its knowledge capacity. The problem, however, is that this has not been an enhancement designed to improve knowledge about trade and the multilateral trading system *per se* but rather to rescue the institution from a perceived loss of credibility caused by the Doha negotiations and to preserve the institution as a distinct entity by distancing (if not wholly divorcing) it from the political shenanigans of the current (and no doubt future) round(s). The result has been to enhance the generation of research that speaks to this purpose and not knowledge about trade and the multilateral trading system more objectively conceived.

Despite this instrumental start, the enhancement of the WTO's technical capacity provides a solid foundation upon which a genuinely cutting-edge programme of trade and development innovation can occur. This programme could be tailored towards much more nuanced and country-specific knowledge production which could then be disseminated as technical assistance that moves far beyond the plug-and-play capacity building programmes that all too frequently prevail. Such an endeavour would require substantial funding – which the secretariat could cover by charging for its services on a sliding scale, with the least developed paying nothing (or at most a nominal fee) and the largest trading nations paying the most – but the benefits for all members would be real and tangible thereby justifying the fee. Not only would knowledge of the system be improved, in developing discrete and tailored country-specific programmes that are consistent with the achievement of the institution's new aims each member would benefit from bespoke attention. The idea would be that these programmes build upon and help take forward the knowledge capacity of each member, rather than be a rival.

Conclusion

We did not always think in narrow and myopic ways about trade. Our view of what a trade organization is and does has simply been lost in the translation of time. Nonetheless, we have an opportunity to start afresh. What is required is that the moment is seized and a new course charted. The priority is the convening of a conference akin to that which the ILO held in Philadelphia in 1944 and the task at hand to adjust what it is that the WTO does. This reorientation should treat social outcomes as the first-order concern and not as a second-order consequence of market opening; and it is on this basis that the performance of a refashioned WTO should be assessed. Reorienting the WTO around a development-for-all agenda that moves away fundamentally from competitive negotiating as the mechanism by which governance is exercised offers not only the capacity to contribute to making the world a better place but also a reform path that would preserve the institution in the face of continuing stalemate and pressure. That said, my purpose in this chapter has been merely to outline some of what a fundamentally reoriented organization should and could comprise as well as how it might be governed. There are two questions I have not yet addressed. The first is what should the WTO do in the interim – that is, what would a more progressive work programme look like in the short term? The second is how do we get from where we are to where we should be going? It is to these tasks that the next chapter turns.

CHAPTER SIX

Getting from here to there

How do we get from where we currently are to where we should be going? We certainly should not dispatch the organization, abandoning existing structures in one fell swoop and with it what global trade governance we actually have. Equally, we should be wary that in all institutions, irrespective of whether self-reflective programmes of reform have been confected and pursued, old ways of thinking and operating remain engrained and are hard to overcome. Yet, we also need to recognize that while these old ways of thinking and operating are part of the problem they can also be part of the solution. In crafting an ILO-style Philadelphia moment for the WTO, for instance, involving those people that are the everyday of the organization is essential. This involvement should be constructed in such a way that resort to existing ways of thinking and acting is restrained. The secretariat has a view, as do many outside the organization, along with all of the member states. All of these views need to be aired even if they cannot all be accommodated. They need to be expressed in front of those who will lead the redesign of the WTO. And those who lead the redesign should not be the usual body of suspects that sit on one consultative group or another discussing similar issues and arriving at known and ultimately uninspiring solutions. Rather, they should comprise and accommodate as broad a swathe of interests as possible.

The same is also true for the negotiating mechanism that lies at the heart of the problem. While this part of the institution does need to be dispatched, it has a utility in the short to medium term that can be usefully realized. To bring about any substantive change in the WTO requires that members agree to such change (and the substance of that change be negotiated). Certainly, the GATT/WTO has brought significant advantages to the leading industrial states. And while it is the case that any conclusion of the Doha round is likely to bring about yet another asymmetrical bargain (as the Bali package foreshadows), the effort required to reach a conclusion and extent to which the system has ground to a halt has created a moment wherein substantive change has become a possibility. Whatever happens, the WTO cannot continue to operate in the way it has. To do so would consign the organization to irrelevance. So, a way forward needs to be contrived that maps out changes which slowly but steadily alter what it is that the WTO does, that result in a refreshing and reorientation of the organization in way that also speaks to the interests of all the organization's members, which utilizes what means are currently available, but which in the longer term results in a radical transformation.

My purpose in this chapter is to set out how through a programme of reform the orientation of the WTO can be adjusted and the purpose of the organization transformed into one wherein trade-led development-for-all is the driving objective. The emphasis here is on reform in discrete stages utilizing existing capacities as a way forward. The proposals are intended to be reasonable propositions that could form the basis of a programme of change as well as a discussion about the future of the WTO with the purpose of radically transforming – in the aggregate – the way we govern global trade.

The chapter unfolds as follows. It begins by exploring the necessity of constructing a new trade narrative as a precursor to any programme of reform. Here the chapter considers how and why adjustments must be made in the way we think and talk about trade before meaningful reform can be realized. Thereafter, the chapter considers the utility of *increasing* rather than narrowing the arena of public debate on trade issues and the positive spill-overs this would have for the reform debate by instigating a grand global economic forum. In this section, the chapter explores not only the benefits of broad-based conversations with a variety of stakeholders in terms of institutional transparency and account-ability, but also their usefulness as venues for the development of new and novel ideas. The chapter then considers how the WTO's existing machinery can be mobilized to operate in ways that begin to speak to a more progressive social agenda enabling trade gains for all to be realized.

Talking and thinking better about trade

Trade has an extraordinary capacity to produce good and gener-ate harm. It can produce good when rules and regulations enable producers to get their products into markets fairly. It can gen-erate harm when markets are controlled in ways that speak to vested and special interests, to the detriment of others. Trade can bring about genuine cultural interchange, attaching to goods and services consumed in places far from their points of production information about alternative ways of organizing social life. Trade generates harm when the transportation and sale of hazardous goods and services are not heavily restricted – if not rendered impossible – or when producers are brought into exploitative relationships with buyers. Very little of this has to do with an abstract idea of what we consider a market to be, but it has a great deal to do with how we construct the environments in which we allow economic behaviour to take place – in other words, the *kind* of markets we create.

Markets are merely constructed and institutionalized forms of exchange. Their character is determined by the myriad rules, regulations, practices, procedures and norms that emerge from the ideas we have about trade as well as social life more broadly and which affect transactions taking place therein. Some forms of market regulation are specific to individual contexts, others are more universally agreed. Trade in those goods and services that we consider to be noxious (enriched plutonium, body parts, people, mercenary services, sex work on so on) are heavily restricted, controlled or banned. Trade outside what we deem as society's established parameters is illegal and sanctions likely to be forthcoming. Other goods and services are less heavily controlled but the rules that govern that trade nonetheless have an effect on what is traded, how it is traded, who trades and what is exchanged. Some of these rules confer on the holders of intellectual property rights an exclusive or near exclusive right to trade in a particular good, others require consumers to have specific attributes (for example, that they are over a particular age to purchase and consume alcohol), others still limit the quantity of goods and services that can be bought in particular settings (such as duty-free allowances).

The character of markets is not only determined by what we trade or how we regulate that trade. It also results from the ideas we have about the outcomes to which particular forms of exchange give rise. We have long appreciated that markets can be regulated in ways that are socially beneficial and sought to regulate the type and amount of particular goods being traded by allowing only some producers and consumers to participate, and by controlling supply and demand. Tobacco, alcohol and pharmaceutical markets are, for instance, regulated in ways that pursue certain social outcomes such as improved life expectancy and rates of morbidity.

Yet, we seem unable to make the leap between understanding the socially progressive way markets can be regulated and the necessity of constructing broad global frameworks of rules that enable the totality of 'normal' trade (that is, the vast majority of goods and services traded and which are not for good reason controlled or restricted) to serve wider social purposes. We know that the way the multilateral trading system has operated has created an enabling environment for some producers in some countries while discriminating against other producers in other countries. Yet we have failed to connect this acknowledgement up with the necessity of creating a global framework of rules that provides an enabling environment that is equitable and which promotes development-for-all. We know part of the problem lies in the way the multilateral trading system has evolved – that is, we have persisted with the construction of a global trading environment using a tool that is fit only for particularist purposes. We also know that part of the problem lies in our tendency to treat the GATT/WTO and the liberalization that has taken place under its auspices as synonymous with social progress and to see attacks on the multilateral trading system as assaults on free or freer trade (and what we imagine the entailments greater trade freedom may bring). We have been wrong about the way we regulate markets before and we as a global community have woken up to this fact and done something about it (with varying degrees of success it should be noted). Yet, we seem only willing to reconstitute some markets, but not to do this for the global trading system. We are, for instance, no longer willing to allow a permissive environment to exist wherein 'innovation' in financial products can spiral out of control resulting in system-wide crisis (as we did before the 2007–8 subprime crisis), so why would we stand back and do nothing to address the regulatory failures in a system of global trade governance that allows those who already have to thrive at the expense of those who do not?

As Dani Rodrik observes with regard to global finance, and which could equally be applied to the global trading system:

> our basic narrative has lost it credibility and appeal. It will be quite some time before any policy maker can be persuaded that financial innovation is an overwhelming force for good, that financial markets are best policed through self-regulation, or that governments can expect to let large financial institutions pay for their own mistakes. We need a new narrative to shape the next stage of globalization. The more thoughtful that new

> narrative, the healthier our economies will be. (Rodrik, 2011: xiii)

We cannot hope that a new trade (or global economic) narrative will appear organically from the ether. We have to actively construct one. We need to do this with urgency and utilize the moment that the general hiatus in the Doha round affords and the momentum generated by the Bali agreement. We need to be aware that status quo-preserving narratives legitimizing what it is that the WTO does are driving others – particularly the secretariat – to develop alternative narratives which present real challenges to the realization of a new trade order. We need to avoid hackneyed expressions, recycled commentary, crisis politics and the tendency to attribute blame. We need a collective realization that new and fundamentally reformed institutions are required at multiple levels (global, regional, national and local) to create opportunities for all and compensate for past and future losses where appropriate. Moreover, we need a new language and arena of exchange in which to express and debate ideas.

Moreover, we need a genuine debate about the social purpose of trade and a global trade institution conducted in an open, transparent and democratic fashion. We need this debate to focus on what the WTO is for as well as how (and which) trade rules should shape global markets to enable them to produce the outcomes that we agree upon. We need to ignite this conversation so that it flourishes ahead of an ILO-style Philadelphia moment designed to reorient the WTO. We need to involve in this conversation as many stakeholders as possible. And one conceivable way of doing this, as well as to ensure that ideas are continually debated and refreshed while at the same time expanding the institution's legitimacy and accountability credentials, is to put in place a grand global economic forum.

A grand global economic forum

Public interest in economic issues continues unabated despite a marked fall-back in attendance at WTO and other intergovernmental conferences in recent years. The secretariat's effort to take the politics out of the ministerial conference and of the public forum is not the right move. Despite the interruptions to proceedings that a handful of NGO activities may have generated during particularly volatile ministerial conferences (Wilkinson, 2003; 2006b), the decision to let civil society actors take part in these events was widely welcomed in grassroots debate. The seriousness with which public forums took issues of civil society engagement prior to the 2013 event did likewise. Both the NGO aspects of the ministerial conference and the public forum have also been important sites for developing country delegations to gain access to information they have otherwise found hard to find while also giving them access to a large collection of groups interested in development issues.

These fora thus serve an important function in their capacity to bring excluded voices together. Their capacity to ignite dialogue and to share knowledge suggests that rather than being constrained or scaled-back they should be allowed to flourish. Indeed, reconstituting the public forum into a wider civil society and other stakeholder event would provide the basis upon which a broader conversation about the purpose and value of the WTO could be begun and which could feed into the preparatory process for a wider conference on the future of the institution.

One of the complaints civil society organizations often have about existing events, however, has been that they are a little too narrowly focused on specific trade issues and not connected up to other global economic debates. This could be easily addressed not only by expanding the scope of debate but also by combining public meetings on trade with those of other organizations – particularly those who are also at the forefront of public anxiety about the governance of the global economy (principally, but not exclusively, the IMF and World Bank) – and creating a grand global economic forum. The hosting of a grand annual public event wherein debate and discussion takes place would not only recapture some of the loss of credibility caused by the recent re-engineering of the WTO's image, it would offer civil society actors an important venue in which to engage with global institutions as well as with each other. It would serve as a solid foundation upon which to build a Philadelphia-style conference like the ILO's. And it would be an event from which delegations (particularly from developing countries but also from industrial states) could also benefit.

Organizations like the WTO should not step away from their responsibilities here. Existing fora are not sufficient substitutes for such a public event – though much can be learnt from studying their experiences (see Teivainen, 2002; Graz, 2003; Peña and Davis, 2013; Elias, 2013) – nor are they the sole institutions with which civil society organizations wish to engage. The World Economic Forum (WEF), for example, is designed to bring major corporate actors together with government officials allowing policy discussions at the highest and most exclusive level. The closest the WEF gets to public engagement is by delivering its message in a unidirectional fashion via the various virtual means its website allows. Likewise, the World Social Forum (WSF) is also insufficient in this regard. The lack of seriousness with which, and constructive engagement in, the WSF by policymaking elites excludes it as a serious forum for bringing a wide variety of actors together in debate and dialogue.

Certainly, an initiative like a grand global economic forum has the capacity to be both vast and out of control, particularly as its purpose should be to let the proverbial 100 flowers blossom in a genuinely open venue. Yet, this is not beyond our wit to work out and manage. Any headaches that this would bring would be made irrelevant by the capacity of such a forum to bring excluded voices – often those most affected by the consequences of policies developed in, and operationalized by, global economic organizations – into a broader conversation and to have these feed into the process by which the WTO is reoriented.

It is important that efforts to control strongly the agenda of events like these, as well as determine just who has a legitimate interest in trade and/or global economic issues (as the NGO-registration process of WTO ministerial conferences does), should be resisted. Agendas should not be engineered to depoliticize events but rather to encourage debate. Certainly, broad themes should be established to lend a structure to discussions, but these should be decided in concert with civil society representatives (perhaps in what could be the forerunner of a stakeholder assembly discussed in Chapter 5). And while there will inevitably be difficulties in its establishment, the appropriate way to set the tone of these events should be through an advisory panel comprised of multiple constituents – state, secretariat, civil society, business and so on.

Of course there are very real dangers in a grand global economic forum becoming mere public theatre, a place for sharing and expressing anxiety, knowledge and ideas but which sits in front of – and actually acts as a bulwark against – the real machineries of power. Equally, the mere existence of a grand global economic forum should not, by itself, be allowed to generate a myth that civil society concerns are being listened to. Real forms of engagement need to take place otherwise such a forum would lack any credibility.

These kinds of criticisms have been levelled at the grand global summits before. We need think no further than the environmental summits held under UN auspices – Rio, Kyoto, Copenhagen, Johannesburg. It is easy to see why. Despite the great hope that they might generate serious and concerted action, they have been much derided for the meagreness of their achievements and the feebleness with which they have been able to bind states to what at root are rather unambitious targets. The same could be said for grand economic summits like the UN Millennium Summit as well as for (what some consider) a lacklustre set of policy prescriptions that have evolved therefrom (the Millennium Development Goals – MDGs) (see, for instance, Harcourt, 2005). These summits do, however, have great significance. They help accelerate the process by which international norms – around the necessity to combat climate change and reduce poverty for instance (Fukuda-Parr and Hulme, 2011; Fukuda-Parr, 2012) – are disseminated, gather steam and come to have an effect on state and non-state behaviour; they keep issues in the foreground and establish a terrain on which a political agenda can be recaptured; and they offer a place wherein non-state and not-for-profit interests can be expressed.

This latter point is perhaps the most instructive. The democratic credibility, legitimacy and accountability of all of our global economic institutions have been repeatedly called into question. It has never been enough – as in the case of the WTO – to point to an assertion that the organization's one-member-one-vote system of decision-making is the basis of its democratic credentials when voting never occurs and decisions are made on the basis of confected consensus. Equally, it is a nonsense to suggest that just because sovereign states join global institutions these world bodies are accountable. A grand global economic forum could become a way of expressing concerns about, as well as facilitating forms of engagement with what global economic government we actually have, irrespective of the theatrical role it may serve (see Death, 2011: 2).

We should also bear in mind here that the idea is not to repeat or replicate Rio or Kyoto but rather to establish a grand forum that has political engagement around issues of progressive global public policy as a core purpose. Out of events such as these naturally flow consequences. This is the point of creating environments that facilitate the exchange of information and knowledge and which encourage debate. While the idea of putting something together that offers civil society groups a chance to engage with our major global economic institutions may be irksome to some, it would go a considerable way to democratizing what global economic governance we actually have. We should take a leaf out of the UN's experience in this regard.

Whether the Fund, the Bank and the WTO choose to co-operate with one another or not in a venture such as this, they cannot remain aloof from the broader constituencies that they are supposed to serve (and here I mean ordinary people not diplomatic and policy elites). Equally, in establishing such a forum none of the institutions (secretariats, member states and centrally engaged parties) can choose to engage only at the margins. This has to be a genuine conversation as out of genuine conversations spring new and novel ideas. One of the problems that the trade-policy elite has is that everyone knows each other, they all talk with one another regularly, and they can and do circulate and recirculate versions of tired and hackneyed ideas. Opening up a conversation to a new community will inevitably take debates in directions that are hitherto unknown. Not only will this break the unhealthy dominance that the policymaking elite has over ideas about how to govern trade (which have clearly not been working for some time), it will encourage us to talk about trade in different ways unencumbered by the exclusionary language, linguistic sleights of hand, metaphorical cul-de-sacs and accusatory politics that have become so tiresome. In engaging in this way we may just find that constructive knowledge and ideas are found in unusual places; and by bringing new groups and generations into a conversation a constant process of reflection and stimulation will take place.

What is the WTO good for?

To get us from where we are to where we need to go requires that we do more than just rethink the way we think and talk about trade or set the foundations of a grand conversation. We also have to show how the trade machinery we currently have can be utilized in a way that is productive as well as consistent with the overarching goal of fundamentally transforming the way we govern global trade. Simply pursuing piecemeal reform will not do. One of the benefits of utilizing the WTO as it currently exists is that it provides an already existing forum in which trade issues can be negotiated, in which sunk costs have been invested and wherein a measure of credibility exists. It brings trade officials together in reasonably regularized sessions to debate issues of trade. The challenge is to restrict the capacity of the institution to revert to type and not fall back on known, existing and problematic ways of operating. Nonetheless, to radically transform the institution requires at a minimum that members buy into a process that has the potential to produce a different organization. The growing consensus on the need to reflect upon the functioning of the WTO in the Doha round offers an important foothold upon which to embark on this exercise.

Moving forward in bite-sized but focused pieces

Imagining that the WTO or the multilateral trading system can change overnight is of course folly. Yet the institution's pre-existing negotiating capacity could certainly be utilized to move the organization in a different direction in discrete, interconnected and realizable stages. The key – and first stage – is to have a coherent agenda that is commonly agreed upon and in which all interests have been equitably represented. A second stage would then be to use the negotiating machinery to launch discussions on bite-sized thematic issues that move from one issue to another, which are not tied in with trade-offs in other areas, and which do not fall foul of the problems of plurilaterals or other forms of mini-lateral politics.

To be clear, this is not a suggestion to begin a new round. Quite the contrary. Rounds as a form of negotiating should be abolished. Rather, what should unfold in their stead are dis-crete negotiations on issues that are of broad concern *and* which genuinely begin addressing the imbalance in the distribution of opportunity among members but which are also part of an ongoing process that works through an agenda agreed by the General Council and which moves through a known sequence of areas each of which speaks – and indeed is required to show its contribution – to broader social objectives as well as the longer-term goal of fundamental transformation.

What could the contenders be for these more easily digest-ible negotiations? The first and least contentious ought to be the negotiation of a more *enabling environment for least-developed countries* that builds upon but which also moves a considerable way beyond the provisions of the December 2013 Bali package. The giving away of enhanced market-access concessions by *all* WTO members in *all* areas to LDCs coupled with various safe-guard mechanisms ought to be a first stage. These enhanced concessions ought to be provided on the basis that they would be reviewed in the future on the understanding that preferential treatment is not an in-perpetuity right but rather a form of short- to medium-term assistance. The *quid pro quo* here, however, is that the preferential treatment agreed has to be meaningful and substantive and connected up with assistance programmes that are themselves substantive and tailored to the specific develop-ment needs of each of the countries in question. In addition this package ought to be connected up with wider agendas that seek to improve the lot of LDCs – such as the Istanbul Programme of Action for Least-developed Countries (UN, 2011) – but which emphasize more than just improvements in per capita income levels as evidence of sustainable development trajectories (Bhattacharya and Borgatti, 2012).

A second subject for discussion could be the establishment of an *Aid for Trade Fund*. The purpose of this fund would be to aggregate financial assistance for trade-capacity building and to manage its distribution more effectively. The benefits of this system are set out in the lengthier discussion in the previous chapter, but the transparency that this would lend to trade-related overseas assistance, the economies of scale that could be achieved, the creation of greater efficiencies through the removal of double counting, the targeted interventions, and the requirement that the assistance contributions are 'real' as opposed to 'phantom' (Bhattacharya, 2009) are compelling in themselves. The fund could be used to begin the move away from treating members as the primary focus to areas and economic sectors that cut across countries. From the outset, the fund should actively seek to address trade-related problems in developed and developing countries as well as in their least-developed counterparts. The key here is not only living up to the intentions of this fund but also being seen to be doing so. This is particularly important to ensure that developed members buy into the system.

A third relatively straightforward thematic negotiation could be to seek agreement on *up-scaling the technical capacity of the secretariat*. The negotiations would be directed at securing a mandate for a significant enhancement of the knowledge and technical assistance aspects of the secretariat's work but in a way that supports the achievement of a development-for-all mandate and not to preserve the organization in its current state. A key part of this strategy would be to involve the work of the secretariat more with other international organizations. The work with the OECD on measuring added-value – while problematic in itself – illustrates well the benefits of inter-institutional co-operation of this sort. Bringing the WTO's capacity together with that of UNCTAD while at the same time moving the work of the ITC more 'in-house' would also be useful in this regard.

A fourth, more substantive area would be to put in motion a wholesale reform of the system through a thorough review of the *Functioning of the World Trade Organization*. This is where the foundations could be laid for a grand reflective exercise

Table 6.1. Countries in the process of acceding to the WTO (as of December 2013)	
Afghanistan	Iraq
Algeria	Kazakhstan
Andorra	Lebanon
Azerbaijan	Liberia
Bahamas	Libya
Belarus	São Tomé and Príncipe
Bhutan	Serbia
Bosnia and Herzegovina	Seychelles
Comoros	Sudan
Equatorial Guinea	Syria
Ethiopia	Uzbekistan
Iran	

Source: List of members registered as observer governments at the WTO minus the Holy See which is not required to begin accession negotiations. See http://www.wto. org/english/thewto_e/whatis_e/tif_e/org6_e.htm

reorientating the focus of the organization, a review of its governance, and the establishment of a (new and different) governing
council and stakeholder assembly, the setting up of substantive public-engagement machineries (such as the grand global
economic forum), and discussions relating to the overlapping
mandates and need to streamline and harmonize the capabilities of trade institutions horizontally and vertically, among other
things. A FOWTO exercise would also provide an opportunity to
build upon the inter-institutional co-operation nurtured by the
upscaling of the secretariat's technical assistance capacity, target
the elimination of institutional overlap and double counting, and
explore moments for deeper co-operation and potential merger.

A fifth area would be to embark on negotiations on *accession*.
The idea here would be to agree a blanket accession regime cov-
ering all of those countries in the queue to join the WTO (see
Table 6.1) designed to accelerate membership and to overcome

the expensive and untoward aspects of the current procedures. All of the countries in the queue are small, developing and/or fragile economies. Many have been in the process of acceding for more than fifteen years. None are significant in terms of their overall share of world trade. Many suffer from a lack of expertise and struggle with the sheer financial costs of negotiating accession. All could be offered membership on undemanding terms in a manner akin to the mass accession that occurred in 1994 ahead of the WTO's creation. This would go some way to ensuring that almost all states were members of the WTO ahead of a fundamental reorientation of the organization in which all of their views would need to be represented.

Thereafter the negotiations could move to consider *discrete thematic negotiations on market access*. This could begin with a focus on something relatively uncontroversial such as e-commerce (perhaps codifying the existing position of 'holding steady' while at the same time negotiating special measures for those least able to engage in virtual markets). Thereafter, the negotiations could move through issues such as intellectual property rights (perhaps agreeing time limits for intellectual property rights on life-saving drugs) and government procurement to thornier but essential issues such as services and agriculture. Other areas could be targeted for improvement such as dispute settlement, trade-policy review and the monitoring of sub-multilateral trade agreements (that is, all forms of bilateral, regional and plurilateral preferential agreements) particularly with a view to enabling developing countries to participate on an equal footing. Nonetheless, the key would be to construct the negotiations so that they are inclusive and which speak to the wider (newly constituted) goals of the organization, not an expansion in the volume and value of trade as an end in itself.

What would these negotiations comprise? The key here is sequencing, both in terms of the issues tackled and the commitments they generate. With regard to the sequence of issues, the idea would be to build up a head of steam in thematic negotiations by moving from those issues wherein agreement is most likely to be forthcoming to those that are more difficult. Establishing a clearly visible agenda with cast-iron agreement that issues of interest to all members (developed and developing alike) will be discussed in a knowable sequence will be important for ensuring that all members buy into the system.

Commitment-wise, it makes sense – particularly in thorny areas – to agree a clear time-frame in which measures will be implemented. So, in agriculture for instance, the removal of the vast subsidy regimes of the United States and the European Union (not to mention in many other countries) is essential but unlikely in the long run. Having clearly defined phase-out dates could be a core component of these negotiations but these dates would have to come with two clear provisos. First, subsidies (or whatever trade-distorting measure is being phased out) should be wound down progressively in knowable stages over time. This would enable subsidy receivers an 'ease in' period while also beginning the process of opening up agricultural markets to foreign producers earlier than a defined future point. Second, a compensatory mechanism should be introduced wherein a financial transfer is made to injured parties in the event that subsidies are not wholly or partially phased out by a specified date. This would not only act as an incentive to the subsidy provider to ensure that their regimes are indeed brought into line with any agreement and provide compensation to injured parties, the monitoring of these regimes and their enforcement could be handed over to the WTO. Similar timetables could be agreed in but also services, particularly with regard to the free movement of people, in intellectual property (perhaps in relation to geographical indicators and points at which compulsory licensing could be issued), and in the relaxation/reconstitution of rules of origin.

The keys to this thematic agenda are surety and visibility. Members, particularly developed countries who will need reason to buy into a process that sees measures designed to help least-developed and developing countries negotiated first, will need to know that a fair agenda has been agreed with all interests equitably represented and that it will be *followed without derogation or renegotiation*. They will also require that the negotiations are transparent, inclusive and representative, and that the commitment to progress through an agenda is adhered to by all.

These are all, however, first measures. In themselves they will not radically transform the institution. Indeed, if they are not attached to a strong commitment to a radical overhaul that has a clear timetable for fundamental reform, the system will be likely to remain intact. The trick here is to blend the progression of these issues with an overhaul of the decision-making procedures. A first step here would be to lay the foundations for a constitutional overhaul of the system creating both a new governing council and a stakeholder assembly (detailed in the previous chapter). A second step would be to explore and exploit the synergies that exist between the WTO and other trade (and trade-related) institutions with a view not only to utilizing the economies of scale of closer co-operation but also the merger of particular functions, the identification of comparative advantages, and the overall shape of the bureaucracy, its governance and attendant accountability mechanisms (again, detailed in the previous chapter). A third step would be to begin piecing together an arena for stakeholder debate, of which a grand global economic forum would be part.

At the same time arrangements would need to be put in place to begin discussions about the purpose of global trade governance with a view to drafting a statement of aims and objectives that define the system's social purpose, to which trade mechanisms are secondary and subordinate. Allied to this would be the development of a robust monitoring mechanism designed to measure the system's wider social contribution rather than just increases in the volume and value of trade. These measures, in turn, would provide the foundations for a Philadelphia-style conference at which the purpose of the system is agreed and wherein a statement of intent about future development is determined.

Paying for all of this

Reorienting what it is that the WTO does will not come cheaply. Indeed, it should not. The system requires a radical overhaul and serious investment in the development of a trade capacity that actually makes a substantive contribution to making the world a better place. Under-funding a revised system would be a sure-fire way to ensure its failure. It would, nonetheless, have to come from increased subscriptions from member states on that basis that *all* stand to benefit from the improvement in its operations. It is worth underlining once again the importance of a strict plan of sequenced activity. Benefits might not flow to all members in the near term (though one would hope that least-developed countries are at the head of the queue) but clear guarantees that the interests of all will be the concern of the organization – that is, their contributions will be met reciprocally albeit diffusely (that is, in the aggregate and over time) – should be treated as a foundation for buying into the new regime.

The WTO is funded primarily by the contributions of members based on an agreed formula that works out individual contributions relative to a country's respective share of world trade averaged out over a three-year period and mindful of the capacity of a member to contribute. In 2013 this gave the WTO an operating budget of CHF195,500,000 (approximately US $218,755,116).[30] This is a little over one-eleventh of the operating budget of the World Bank[31] (US $2,548,400,000) – though the differences in the size of their staffs are of a different order of magnitude (629 for the WTO compared with more than 9,000 for the World Bank).[32] Raising the size of members' contributions would clearly be a first step but the economies of scale that could be achieved by bringing together the various global institutions with trade mandates – and the subscriptions members pay to each – would offset the increases and remove any double counting and operational repetition. Rationalizing the management of all other sub-multilateral trading agreements (that is, all bilateral and regional RTAs), including the subscriptions that members pay to each, would add financial value to the wider goals of monitoring and co-ordinating these arrangements.

A timetable for reform

The hardest task is to establish when this should happen and how long it should take. Despite proclamations to the contrary, too much has already been invested in the Doha round for any of the leading players to be genuinely willing to abandon the negotiations. The plurilateral renaissance has probably ensured that some form of agreement will be reached but it will certainly not be the single undertaking that was originally envisaged or the conclusion of a substantively development-focused round irrespective of members' capacity to agree to a multilateral package in Bali. Assuming that this is likely to be the case, two options present themselves, with the first being preferable to the second.

Option one is to begin reorienting the organization in tandem with what passes for the DDA. This could be done under the auspices of a FOWTO agenda with a view to agreeing an agenda that begins the process of reform. The second option is to wait until after the Doha round is concluded. Neither option is ideal as it accepts that some element of agreement will be reached in the course of the DDA, and this is not likely to speak to the new development-for-all focus that the organization should have. Option two is the more problematic. With option one, a substantive reform agenda would be able to capitalize on the stasis in the round while at the same time building on the desire of all members to salvage something from the DDA. Option two, however, would not be able to benefit from such a moment. Moreover, the conclusion of yet another asymmetrical bargain may well damage the system to such an extent that the desire of any of the members to get back to the table anytime soon would be severely limited. This would, in turn, push reform of the institution back into the medium term long beyond the point after which the DDA is concluded – which, on current projections, could be a very long time indeed.

Conclusion

Working out how we get from where we are to where we ought to be is the harder of the tasks of these two final chapters. Putting forward reasonable proposals for what a world trade organization ought to look like is easy compared with trying to work out how it can and should happen. Nonetheless, two final points require making. First, no reform agenda is going to take place without significant buy-in and willingness from the membership. This is particularly so with regards to the developed countries as they appear to have the most to lose (but only if we assume that the system could continue to produce the asymmetrical bargains from which they have consistently benefited which, in the face of evidence that suggests it is more likely to grind to a halt, looks unlikely). Second, reform of the system requires enlightened leadership. This leadership may come from a member state willing to move the agenda forward and craft a new multilateral trade order. It may also be the case that enlightened leadership comes from a WTO DG concerned with the past and future direction of the organization and willing to drive forward a radically different agenda. From wherever it comes, without brave leadership – and it should be said serious and committed followership – the system risks spinning into further atrophy and irrelevance.

Conclusion:
Moving beyond the state we are in

Almost a century ago John Maynard Keynes recognized our capacity to regard institutions as if they were unalterable facts of nature and to act as if we could not effect change. As he put it:

> The power to become habituated to his surroundings is a marked characteristic of mankind. Very few of us realize with conviction the intensely unusual, unstable, complicated, unreliable, temporary nature of the economic organization by which Western Europe has lived for the last half century. We assume some of the most peculiar and temporary of our late advantages as natural, permanent, and to be depended on, and we lay our plans accordingly. (Keynes, 1920: 1)

Keynes' lesson was that we fail to act upon changes – material, ideational and otherwise – and to reform our institutions accordingly, at our peril. While his task was to stop Europe and (to a lesser extent) North America from sleep-walking into the problems the Paris Peace accords would inevitably bring, his warning has wider and longer-lasting resonance. We run the risk of observing the problems of the WTO in a similarly unconscious way. We treat what global trade governance we have as if it were immoveable, able to be altered in appearance (but not substance) alone. We do not ask what the point of a world trade organization is or what purposes it should serve. We blind ourselves with commonsense assumptions that treat the institution and free and freer trade as synonyms. And we resign ourselves to treating the symptoms of institutional malaise rather than their root cause. In so doing, we leave intact a system that is fundamentally unfit for purpose, which fails to distribute economic opportunities equitably particularly to those who need them most, and which is becoming increasingly encased in a quagmire from which there appears to be little possibility of escape.

Yet, this is not the full extent of the problems with which we are faced. It is not always obvious once we have realized that change is required, how it can actually be brought about. Precisely because institutions are treated as immoveable monoliths, we often resign ourselves to the impossibility of change. We look for examples of how it can be brought about, or explanatory frameworks that guide change. Institutional theory tells us that moments akin to the one in which the WTO finds itself – crisis points in an institution's evolution – can be as much opportunities as they are problems. They can result in reversions to type through concerted efforts to preserve an institutional form (akin to what the secretariat is currently doing), generate well-meaning (or otherwise) but nonetheless piecemeal reform (as Chapter 4 shows), or else they can produce opportunities that if appropriately seized can produce fundamental departures from existing ways of operating (explored in Chapter 5). Equally, institutional theory tells us that the sum of ongoing incrementalism – that is, discrete changes in an institution's functioning – can result, in the aggregate, in dramatic change (a strategy examined in Chapter 6); or else it can reinforce existing ways of thinking and acting.

The problem with reforming global institutions is that change is almost always incremental. In the case of the WTO – and almost all of the intergovernmental organizations that we have – the changes that have been attempted have been in keeping with existing norms and ways of operating. With the possible exception of the ILO (about which an argument can be made either way) rarely do our international organizations change radically. Indeed, radical change in international organizations has more often than not been associated with catastrophic demise (as was the case with the League of Nations) than it has with a fundamental departure from what it is that an institution was set up to achieve.

In large measure this is because our international organizations exist within, are bound up with, and are organically connected to particular global relations of power. When global relations of power are stable, institutions endure; when they are not, as they were not after the First World War, the institutions tied to those relations falter – as was the case with the League. The institutions set up after the Second World War – the UN System, the GATT/WTO and so on – are all reflections of *Pax Americana*. Each was the product of the United States's rise to power; all embodied rules that enabled that rise to be consolidated; they embedded US ideas about how states should behave and how the world economy should function and be organized (if they did not they fell by the wayside, as the case of the ITO clearly shows); and they socialized other states into that system by offering them concessions in return for their acquiescence (Cox, 1983: 171–2). Moreover, they have all endured in a period of relative and indeed growing stability in global-power relations.

It is only when there is a fundamental shift in global-power relations that dramatic institutional change follows. Yet, this is a change *of* institutions rather than a change *in* institutions, as the transition across three distinct periods of global power – *Pax Britannica*, the inter-imperial period, and *Pax Americana* – illustrates. We can observe this in the movement from the Concert of Europe and the International Public Unions, through the League of Nations, to the UN System.

We would thus seem to be limited to understanding institutional change as a consequence of fundamental shifts in global power relations and confining that change to the creation of new institutions. This is not, however, the case; nor is a fundamental shift in global power relations likely to occur anytime soon. This appears to run contrary to existing wisdom, however, and to contradict what we commonly understand to be occurring in world politics. This claim requires a little more elaboration.

For many, global-power relations *are* indeed changing and this may foretell of a changing global order. I am sceptical however. I am sceptical about the result not of the fact that a rearrangement of some of the global furniture is occurring. All of the evidence suggests that while 'new' powers are 'emerging' (an awkward term that many have rightly criticized – see Turner, 2009) they are playing by the rules and being socialized into existing norms and ways of behaving. This is system-preserving behaviour and not the stuff of radical transformation. And while it may be the case that new powers have, can and do rise to the top, the decline of old powers can be a millennial process – witness the role that former European imperial powers continue to play in world politics, whether as notable individuals (as the UK and France are) or as members of the wider European Union. One of the reasons why this decline is slow is precisely because new powers often need the support of old ones (they may no longer have a preponderance of resources or capacity but the old guard none-theless remain formidable) and this need is reflected in the way power relations are institutionalized. Witness the original ITO and GATT negotiations, ostensibly a conversation among sixty states but actually the result of bilateral discussions between the USA and the UK (see Gardner, 1956) or the way decision-making occurs in the WTO today (in which it is the agreement of the G2 – the United States and European Union – that is the ultimate prerequisite).

The idea that there will be a transformation *in* rather than *of* the existing order appears equally unlikely. None of the states commonly identified as challenging the existing order have engaged in behaviour that is anything other than system-maintaining, irrespective of some of the hyperbolic comments of scholars, practitioners and pundits alike (see Scott and Wilkinson, 2013a: 761–8). Moreover, each of the principal 'rising' powers has problems of its own that suggest that the dramatic rates of economic growth they have experienced may not be sustainable. China's rise is the most spectacular of the 'emerging' powers, having registered dramatic economic growth over the last three decades to secure a position as the second-largest national economy in the world. However, it is equally true that China's development trajectory is unlikely to continue in its current form. Not only has its economic performance tailed off since the late 2000s, China's reliance on export-driven growth has made it vulnerable to the kind of demand slowdown evident in many of the world's industrial economies.

The Chinese government is well aware that dependence on an export-driven model is problematic and has begun attempting to reorient the economy away from an over-reliance on overseas demand to one that also promotes domestic consumption – a reorientation that is a key 'guiding principle' of the twelfth five-year plan. Rapid economic growth has also not been unproblematic and it has masked a number of worrying trends. Inequalities in income and wealth, as well as in other indicators have risen sharply, particularly between rural and urban areas (Li, 2011: 137–8). Illiteracy rates have been rising rather than falling (Huang, 2008: 244–5). Job creation has slowed significantly and has increasingly favoured the better-educated and the young (that is, those who are best placed to take advantage of China's entry into the global economy), while disadvantaging marginal rural areas, the old and the less skilled (Solinger, 2003; Wang, 2000). And growth in personal incomes has also moved from exceeding GDP growth to lagging significantly behind (Huang, 2008: 238).

Equally, although some projections suggest India's economy will be the third largest behind the United States and China by 2030, it too suffers from structural problems (rising inequalities, enduring poverty, poor infrastructure in large parts of the country) that will inevitably slow its long-term rate of growth (it has already slowed) and force it to concentrate on domestic, rather than international, issues. Meanwhile, Brazil and South Africa, though clearly gaining in influence, are at present significant regional, rather than global powers.

It is also worth noting that much of the commentary about 'rising' powers and their impact on the governance of global trade is motivated by fears of Western decline. Certainly, these powers have grown economically at spectacular rates but, as we have seen, questions remain as to the extent to which that growth will continue, as well as about the capacity of that growth to be translated into political power. It is also worth noting that a significant number of countries that have successfully managed the process of development have become 'stuck' at some point in their rise. This is particularly true of previous emerging powers: Australia, Canada, Japan and South Korea. Robert Wade (2010: 152–3) argues that there are fewer 'contenders' to rich-country status now than there were forty years ago. Middle-income countries today, he argues, have become caught in the middle: 'their firms [are] stuck in the relatively low value-added segments of global production chains, unable to break into innovation-intensive activities or into the market for branded products, where the high profits are to be made'. China in particular faces these challenges, irrespective of the successes it has shown so far in handling the challenges thrown up by its rapid economic emergence (Huang, 2008; Hutton, 2007).

That said, imagine for a moment that a change in the existing order *did* occur, that those states that are currently on the rise were to supplant the United States and the European Union as the dominant global powers (which is a leap of faith on many fronts but also because a change *in* the order would by necessity require that an accommodation with the *ancien régime* was made). Change *in* a regime would by definition preserve the institutions that we currently have and the way they organize relations among states with the caveat that the beneficiaries of those forms of governance would have changed slightly.

The point here is that there appears to be very little to suggest that fundamental change in the WTO (or any of the current crop of global institutions) is going to arrive anytime soon, if at all. This is not a resignation to hopelessness, however. It is merely a realization that we are looking in the wrong place if we imagine that a fundamental (and progressive) change in the WTO will result from changing global relations of power or indeed spring out of the ether. Instead we need to contrive a moment of change and instigate a process of fundamental reform. What I do not mean here is that we should create a global transition of power. Rather, I am suggesting that we need to engineer a fundamental departure from existing ways of governing global trade (as well as in other areas of global life) without worrying about global power transitions. This will require securing, rather than eschewing, the support of the major trading powers, convincing them that root-and-branch reform is in their interest as well as in that of the greater good, and developing clear and plausible ways forward that are legitimate, transparent and democratic.

Whatever happens, this will not be an easy task – though the consequences will be harder if we do not try. If we eschew the task of creating and building an opportunity for reform, and realizing it appropriately, none of our global institutions will be fit for purpose and we will endure in a world where those who have continue to get everything, while the rest fall by the wayside. What history does teach us is that highly unequal societies are inherently unstable. If we do not attenuate this now, then we and the system in which we reside will be likely to spin into atrophy.

Notes

1 This section draws on Wilkinson, 2006a: 22–44; and Wilkinson, 2011: 48–9.
2 A pattern that has been repeated in every round since. See Wilkinson, 2006a.
3 In the first round, 23 of the 23 contracting parties exchanged concessions. In the second round, 33 of the 33 contracting parties did likewise. Thereafter the numbers fall away. In the third round, only 29 of the 33 contracting parties exchanged concessions; in the fourth round, only 22 of the 39 contracting parties did likewise; in the fifth round (the Dillon round), only 22 of the 42 contracting parties exchanged concessions; in the sixth round (the Kennedy round), 37 of the 76 contracting parties exchanged concessions; while in the seventh round (the Tokyo round), just 44 of the 84 contracting parties exchanged concessions.
4 So-called Singapore because they were first raised as desiderata during the 1996 Singapore ministerial conference.
5 http://www.wto.org/english/thewto_e/whatis_e/tif_e/fact2_e.htm
6 See Patterson, 1966 for what is now an old but nevertheless thorough and extensive treatment of applied exceptions to MFN. See also Viner, 1947; Horn and Mavroidis, 2001.
7 See Wilkinson, 2000: 80–114 for a more detailed discussion of these principles.
8 See Michalopoulos, 1999 for an account of developing-country representation up to and including the early WTO years.
9 The so-called 'Cotton Four' C4.
10 Patel quoted in Beattie, 2005.
11 As the WTO explains: 'The "Green Room" is a phrase taken from the informal name of the director-general's conference room. It is used to refer to meetings of 20–40 delegations, usually at the level of heads of delegations. These meetings can take place elsewhere,

such as at Ministerial Conferences, and can be called by the minister chairing the conference as well as the director-general. Similar smaller group consultations can be organized by the chairs of committees negotiating individual subjects, although the term Green Room is not usually used for these.' See http://www.wto.org/english/thewto_e/whatis_e/tif_e/org1_e.htm

12 The 21 were Argentina, Brazil, Burma, Cambodia, Ceylon, Chile, Cuba, Ghana, Haiti, India, Indonesia, Israel, Federation of Malaya, Federation of Nigeria, Pakistan, Peru, Tanganyika, Tunisia, United Arab Republic, Uruguay and Yugoslavia.

13 Private conversation with the author.

14 This section draws on Wilkinson, 2009.

15 Bergsten did not actually use the term 'bicycle' at first, although Jagdish Bhagwati credits him with putting forward the idea. See Bhagwati, 1993: 41.

16 Interview with a member of the Nigerian delegation (anonymous), Hong Kong, 13 December 2005.

17 Comments during press briefing, 15 December 2005, at the WTO Hong Kong ministerial conference.

18 Conversation (anonymous) with the author during the Joint Initiative for Policy Dialogue/Brooks World Poverty Institute Task Force on Trade Meeting, University of Manchester, 2–3 February 2006.

19 Conversation (anonymous) with the author during the Joint Initiative for Policy Dialogue/Brooks World Poverty Institute task force on Trade Meeting, University of Manchester, 2–3 February 2006. Similar views were also expressed in interviews with delegates from Nigeria, Togo, Malawi, Indonesia, Costa Rica, India, Pakistan, Uruguay and Malaysia during the Hong Kong ministerial conference, 13–18 December 2005 and in follow-up telephone interviews in January/February 2006.

20 An idea first put forward as a post-Doha venture and discussed under Mike Moore's tenure as WTO DG – one aspect of which included a shift back to plurilateralism (see de la Calle, 2002; WTO, 2002) – but which has now switched into the main negotiations.

21 See McRae and Thomas, 1983 for a rare in-depth account of the role of the secretariat.

22 For '10 misunderstandings about the WTO' see http://www.wto.org/english/thewto_e/whatis_e/10mis_e/10m00_e.htm For '10 things the WTO can do' see http://www.wto.org/english/thewto_e/whatis_e/10thi_e/10thi00_e.htm

23 Private conversation with Wilkinson, 2 December 2009.
24 This section draws on Scott and Wilkinson, 2012.
25 See http://www.wto.org/english/thewto_e/
    whatis_e/10thi_e/10thio6_e.htm
26 http://www.wto.org/english/thewto_e/whatis_e/wto_dg_stat_e.htm
27 Available at: http://www.ilo.org/dyn/normlex/
    en/f?p=1000:62:0::NO:62:P62_LIST_ENTRIE_
    ID:2453907:NO#declaration
28 See World Bank mission statement available at http://www.
    worldbank.org/en/about (accessed 28 October 2013)
29 See http://www.wto.org/english/res_e/statis_e/itip_e.htm
30 Calculated at prevailing exchange rate 28 October 2013.
31 Gross figure for the financial year 2014 – see World Bank, 2013.
32 WTO figures for stated size of secretariat as of 28 October 2013.
    World Bank staff figures from http://web.worldbank.org/WBSITE/
    EXTERNAL/EXTSITETOOLS/0,,contentMDK:20147466~menuPK
    :344189~pagePK:98400~piPK:98424~theSitePK:95474,00.html#8
    (accessed 28 October 2013)

References

Accominotti, Olivier and Flandreau, Marc (2008), 'Bilateral Treaties and the Most-Favored-Nation Clause: The Myth of Trade Liberalization in the Nineteenth Century', *World Politics*, 60: 2 (January):147–88.

Albin Cecilia (2008), 'Using negotiation to promote legitimacy: an assessment of proposals for reforming the WTO', *International Affairs*, 8: 4: 757–75.

Alcock, Antony (1971), *History of the International Labour Organisation* (London: Macmillan).

Alden, Edward (2013), 'With TPP and TTIP, US and EU Reassert Control over Rules of Global Trade', *World Politics Review*, 19 December. Available at: http://www.worldpoliticsreview.com/articles/13454/with-tpp-and-ttip-u-s-and-eu-reassert-control-over-rules-of-global-trade

Aliber, Robert Z. (1970), 'Review of *The GATT: Law and International Economic Organization* by Kenneth W. Dam', *University of Chicago Law Review*, 38: 1 (Autumn): 230–3.

Allen, Robert C. (2011), *Global Economic History: A Very Short Introduction* (Oxford: Oxford University Press).

Arreguín-Toft, Ivan (2001), 'How the Weak Win War: A Theory of Asymmetric Conflict', *International Security*, 26: 1 (Summer): 93–128.

Bacchus, James (2003). 'The Bicycle Club: Affirming the American Interest in the Future of the WTO', *Journal of World Trade*, 37: 3: 429–41.

Bagwell, Kyle and Staiger, Robert W. (2002), 'Economic Theory and the Interpretation of GATT/WTO', *American Economist*, 46: 2 (Fall): 3–19.

Barysch, Katinka and Heise, Michael (2014), 'Will TTIP Harm the Global Trading System?', *YaleGlobal Online*, 9 January. Available at: http://yale global.yale.edu/content/will-ttip-harm-global-trading-system

Basra, Hardeep (2012), 'Increased Legalization or Politicalization? A Comparison of Accession under the GATT and WTO', *Journal of World Trade*, 46: 4: 937–59.

Bearce, David H. and Fisher, Eric O'N. (2002), 'Economic Geography, Trade, and War', *Journal of Conflict Resolution*, 46: 3 (June): 365–93.

Beattie, Alan (2005), 'Dipak and the Goliaths', *Financial Times*, 9 December.

—(2009), 'Retread Required', *Financial Times* (Asia edn), 1 December.

Bello, Walden (1999), 'Why Reform of the WTO is the Wrong Agenda', *Focus on Trade*, 43 (December). Available at: http://focusweb.org/publi cations/Books/wto.pdf

Berg, Andrew and Krueger, Anne (2007), 'Lifting All Boats: A Critical Survey of Recent Studies in Trade Liberalization', in Jeremy Clift and Elisa Diehl (eds.), *Financial Globalization: A Compilation of Articles from Finance & Development* (Washington: IMF).

Bergsten, C. Fred (1973), 'Trade Liberalization in Agricultural Products: Future Directions for US Trade', *American Journal of Agricultural Economics*, 55: 2: 280–8.

Bernstein, Steven and Hannah, Erin (2012), 'The WTO and Institutional (In)Coherence in Global Economic Governance', in Amrita Narlikar, Martin Daunton and Robert Stern (eds.), *Handbook on the World Trade Organization* (Oxford: Oxford University Press).

Bhagwati, Jagdish (1993), 'Beyond NAFTA: Clinton's Trading Choices', *Foreign Policy*, 91 (Summer): 155–62.

—(2001) 'After Seattle: Free Trade and the WTO' *International Affairs*, 77: 1: 15–29.

—(2004), 'Don't Cry for Cancún', *Foreign Affairs*, 83: 1 (January/February).

—(2005), 'Reshaping the WTO', *Far Eastern Economic Review*, 168: 2: 25–30.

—(2011), 'The Doha Round's Premature Obituary'. Available at: http://www.project-syndicate.org/commentary/bhagwati12/English

Bhattacharya, Debapriya (2008), 'Ways Forward for the Multilateral Trading System', *Commonwealth Trade Hot Topics*, No. 53 (November).

—(2009), 'Creeping Trade and Phantom Aid: LDCs in the Global Context and Priorities for Reform of Global Governance', text of the *Geneva Lecture on Global Economic Governance* given 29 January 2008 and updated February 2009. Available at: http://www.globaleconomicgov ernance.org/wp-content/uploads/lecture-series-geg-bhattacharya-29-jan-2008.pdf

Bhattacharya, Debapriya and Borgatti, Lisa (2012), 'An Atypical Approach to Graduation from the LDC Category: The Case of Bangladesh', *South Asia Economic Journal*, 13: 1 (March): 1–25.

Breslin, Shaun (2013), 'China and the Global Order: Signalling Threat or Friendship?', *International Affairs*, 89: 3 (May): 615–34.

Bronckers, Marco C. E. J. (2001) 'More Power to the WTO?', *Journal of International Economic Law*, 4: 1: 41–65.

Brooks, Stephen G. and Wohlforth, William C. (2009), 'Reshaping World Order: How Washington Should Reform International Institutions', *Foreign Affairs*, 88: 2 (March/April): 49–63.

Brown, William Adams Jr (1950), *The United States and the Restoration of World Trade* (Washington: Brookings Institution).

Bulmer, Simon and Burch, Martin (1998), 'Organizing for Europe: Whitehall, the British State and European Union', *Public Administration*, 76: 4 (Winter).

Busch, Marc L. and Reinhardt, Eric (2003), 'Developing Countries and General Agreement on Tariffs and Trade/World Trade Organization Dispute Settlement', *Journal of World Trade*, 34: 4: 719–35.

Carr, E. H. (2001), *What is History?* (Basingstoke: Palgrave), 2nd edn.

Chang, Ha-Joon (2007), 'Protectionism . . . The Truth is on a $10 bill', *The Independent* (23 July).

Clapp, Jennifer (2004), 'WTO Agricultural Trade Battles and Food Aid', *Third World Quarterly*, 25: 8.

Clapp, Jennifer and Burnett, Kim (2014), 'Governing Trade in Global Food and Agriculture', in Moschella, Manuela and Weaver, Catherine (eds.), *Handbook of Global Economic Governance: Players, Power and Paradigms* (London: Routledge).

Cooke, Alistair (2007), *American Journey: Life on the Home Front in the Second World War* (London: Penguin).

Copelovitch, Mark S. and Ohls, David (2012), 'Trade, Institutions, and the Timing of GATT/WTO Accession in Post-Colonial States', *Review of International Organizations*, 7: 1 (March): 81–107.

Cornford, Andrew (2004), 'Variable Geometry for the WTO: Concept and Precedents', *UNCTAD Discussion Papers*, No. 171 (May).

Cottier, Thomas (2007), 'Preparing for Structural Reform in the WTO', *Journal of International Economic Law*, 10: 3.

Cox, Robert W. (1973), 'ILO: Limited Monarchy', in Robert Cox and Harold Jacobson et al., *The Anatomy of Influence: Decision Making in International Organizations* (London: Yale University Press).

—(1983), 'Gramsci, Hegemony and International Relations: An Essay in Method', *Millennium: Journal of International Studies*, 12: 2 (June): 162–75.

—(1997), 'Introduction' in Robert W. Cox (ed.), *The New Realism: Perspectives on Multilateralism and World Order* (Basingstoke: Macmillan in association with United Nations University Press).

Cox, Robert W. with Sinclair, Timothy J. (1996), *Approaches to World Order* (Cambridge, Cambridge University Press).

Curzon, Gerard and Curzon, Victoria (1974), 'GATT: Trader's Club', in Robert W. Cox and Harold K. Jacobson (eds.), *The Anatomy of Influence: Decision Making in International Organizations* (London: Yale University Press), 2nd printing.

CUTS (2010), 'Reforming the World Trade Organisation: Developing Countries in the Doha Round', *CUTS Briefing Paper*, No. 2/2010.

—(2013), 'The Multilateral Trading System is Dead: Professor Jagdish Bhagwati', *Press Release*, 27 September.

da Conceição-Heldt, Eugénia (2014), 'Adaptation and Change in EU Trade Governance: The EU's Paradigm Shift from Multilateralism to Regionalism and Bilateralism', in Moschella, Manuela and Weaver, Catherine (eds.), *Handbook of Global Economic Governance* (London: Routledge).

Dam, Kenneth W. (1970), *The GATT: Law and International Economic Organization* (Chicago: Chicago University Press).

de Botton, Alain (2000), *The Consolations of Philosophy* (London: Penguin).

de la Calle, Luis F. (2002), 'The Functioning of the World Trade Organization', paper presented to the WTO Public Symposium on the Doha Development Agenda and Beyond, Geneva (30 April).

Death, Carl (2011), 'Summit Theatre: Exemplary Governmentality and Environmental Diplomacy in Johannesburg and Copenhagen', *Environmental Politics*, 20: 1: 1–19.

Deere-Birkbeck, Carolyn (2009), 'Reinvigorating Debate on WTO Reform: The Contours of a Functional and Normative Approach to Analysing the WTO System', *Global Economic Governance Working Paper*, No. 2009/50 (July), Oxford University.

Dicken, Peter (2011), *Global Shift: Mapping the Changing Contours of the World Economy* (London: Sage), 6th edn.

Diebold Jr, William (1952), 'The End of the ITO', *Essays in International Finance*, 16, International Finance Section, Department of Economics, Princeton University.

Drache, Daniel (2006), 'Trade, Development and the Doha Round: A sure bet or a train wreck?', *Centre for International Governance Innovation Working Paper*, No. 5 (March).

Draper, Peter and Dube, Memory (2013), 'Plurilaterals and the Multilateral Trading System', *Think Piece for the E15 Group on Regional Trade Agreements* (Geneva: ICTSD/IDB). Available at: http://e15initiative.org/wp-content/uploads/2013/08/Draper_E15-RTA_think-piece.pdf

Dresner, Daniel (2014), 'The Contradictions of Post-Crisis Global Economic Governance', in Moschella, Manuela and Weaver, Catherine (eds.), *Handbook of Global Economic Governance* (London: Routledge).

Duffield, Mark (2005), 'Governing the Borderlands: Decoding the Power of Aid', in Rorden Wilkinson (ed.), *The Global Governance Reader* (London: Routledge).

Eagleton-Pierce, Matthew (2012), 'All the Trader's Men: Knowledge and Power in the Field of World Trade', paper presented at *Centre for Research on Socio-Cultural Change (CRESC) Annual Conference: Promises: Crises and Socio-Cultural Change*, University of Manchester, 5–7 September.

—(2013), *Symbolic Power in the World Trade Organization* (Oxford: Oxford University Press).

Economist, The (1999), 'White Man's Shame: Rich Countries Say Free Trade is Good for Poor Countries. Pity They Don't Practice What They Preach', 23 September.

Editorial Board, The (2013), 'A Way to Salvage Global Trade Talks', *New York Times*, 21 October, p. A20 (New York edn).

Elias, Juanita (2013), 'Davos Woman to the Rescue of Global Capitalism: Postfeminist Politics and Competitiveness Promotion at the World Economic Forum', *International Political Sociology*, 7: 2: 152–69.

Elsig, Manfred (2007), 'The World Trade Organization's Legitimacy Crisis', *Journal of World Trade*, 41: 1.

Evans, John W. (1968), 'The General Agreement on Tariffs and Trade', *International Organization*, 22: 1.

—(1971), *The Kennedy Round in American Trade Policy: The Twilight of the GATT?* (Cambridge: Cambridge University Press).

Fairclough, Norman (2001), *Language and Power* (Harlow: Pearson), 2nd edn.

Feis, Herbert (1948), 'The Geneva Proposal for an International Trade Charter', *International Organization*, 2: 1 (February).

Finger, Michael, J. (1991), 'That Old GATT Magic No More Casts Its Spell (How the Uruguay Round Failed)', *Journal of World Trade*, 25: 1 (February).

Finlayson, Jock A. and Zacher, Mark W. (1981), 'The GATT and the Regulation of Trade Barriers: Regime Dynamics and Functions', *International Organization*, 35: 4 (Autumn).

Flowers, Margaret (2013), 'Trans-Pacific Partnership Undermines Health System', *Aljazeera.com*, 17 June. Available at: http://www.aljazeera.com/indepth/opinion/2013/06/201361711230432720.html

Friedman, Thomas (1999), 'Senseless in Seattle', *New York Times*, 1 December.

Fukuda-Parr, Sakiko (2012), 'Recapturing the Narrative of International Development', in Rorden Wilkinson and David Hulme (eds.), *The Millennium Development Goals and Beyond: Global Development after 2015* (London: Routledge).

Fukuda-Parr, Sakiko and Hulme, David (2011), 'International Norm Dynamics and the "End of Poverty": Understanding the Millennium Development Goals', *Global Governance*, 17: 1 (January-March): 17–36.

Gallagher, Kevin P. and Wise, Timothy A. (2009), 'Trading Our Way Out of the Financial Crisis: The Need for WTO Reform', *Americas Policy Brief* (4 March).

Gardner, Richard N. (1956), *Sterling-Dollar Diplomacy: Anglo-American Collaboration in the Reconstruction of Multilateral Trade* (Oxford: Clarendon Press).

—(1964), 'GATT and the United Nations Conference on Trade and Development', *International Organization*, 18: 4 (Autumn).

—(1969), *Sterling-Dollar Diplomacy: The Origins and Prospects of our International Economic Order* (London: McGraw-Hill), 2nd edn.

GATT (1956), *Basic Instruments and Selected Documents: Fourth Supplement* (Geneva: GATT).

—(1962), *Basic Instruments and Selected Documents: Tenth Supplement* (Geneva: GATT).

—(1963), *Basic Instruments and Selected Documents Eleventh Supplement: decisions, reports, etc. of the Twentieth Session* (Geneva: GATT).

—(1986), *Text of the General Agreement on Tariffs and Trade* (Geneva: GATT).

Gilpin, Robert (2001), *Global Political Economy: Understanding the International Economic Order* (Princeton: Princeton University Press).

Gladwell, Malcolm (2006), 'Million-Dollar Murray', *The New Yorker*, 82: 1 (13 February).

Gorter, Wytze (1954) 'GATT after Six Years: An Appraisal' *International Organization*, 8: 1 (February).

Gramsci, Antonio (edited and translated by Quintin Hoare and Geoffrey Nowell Smith) (1998), *Selections from the Prison Notebooks* (London: Lawrence and Wishart).

Graz, Jean-Christophe (2003), 'How Powerful are Transnational Elite Clubs? The Social Myth of the World Economic Forum', *New Political Economy*, 8: 3: 321–40.

Green, Duncan (2011), 'The Doha Round Has Run Its Course But New Trade Realities Demand Solutions'. Available at: http://www.guardian.

co.uk/global-development/poverty-matters/2011/may/04/doha-trade-realities-demand-solutions

Grossman, Gene M. and Helpman, Elhanan (1995), 'Trade Wars and Trade Talks', *Journal of Political Economy*, 103: 4 (August): 675–708.

Guardian, The (2013), 'Leader: Dumping on Doha', 23 June. Available at: http://www.guardian.co.uk/world/2006/jun/23/wto.mainsection?INTCMP=SRCH

Guzman, Andrew T. (2002) 'Global Governance and the WTO', *UC Berkeley Public Law and Legal Theory Research Paper series*, no. 89, 84pp.

Hannah, Erin (2011), 'NGOs and the European Union: Examining the Power of Epistemes in the EC's TRIPS and Access to Medicines Negotiations', *Journal of Civil Society*, 7: 2: 179–206.

Harbinson, Stuart (2011), 'Calls to Pull the Doha Plug Show Naivety not Realism', *Financial Times*, 5 May.

Harcourt, Wendy (2005), 'The Millennium Development Goals: A Missed Opportunity', *Development*, 48: 1: 1–4.

Harrison, Graham (2004), *The World Bank and Africa* (London: Routledge).

Haworth, Nigel, Hughes, Steve and Wilkinson, Rorden (2005), 'The International Labour Standards Regime: A Case Study in Global Regulation', *Environment and Planning A*, 37: 11 (November 2005): 1939–953.

Hayashi, Michiko (2003), 'Arrested Development: Vanuatu's Suspended Accession to the World Trade Organization', case study prepared for the International Commercial Diplomacy Project (February). Available at: http://www.vanuatu.usp.ac.fj/library/Online/Vanuatu/Hayashi.pdf

Heydon, Ken (2006), 'After the WTO Hong Kong Ministerial Meeting: What is at Stake?', *OECD Trade Policy Working Paper*, No. 27.

Heron, Tony (2012), *The Global Political Economy of Trade Protectionism and Liberalization: Trade Reform and Economic Adjustment in Textiles and Clothing* (London: Routledge).

Heron, Tony and Richardson, Ben (2008), 'Path Dependency and the Politics of Liberalisation in the Textiles and Clothing industry', *New Political Economy*, 13: 1 (March): 1–18.

Hines, James R. Jr, Hoynes, Hilary W., Krueger, Alan B. (2001), 'Another Look at Whether a Rising Tide Lifts All Boats', *National Bureau of Economic Research Working Paper*, No. 8412 (August).

Hoekman, Bernard (2011), 'Proposals for WTO Reform: A Synthesis and Assessment', *World Bank Policy Research Working Paper*, No. 5524 (January).

—(2013), 'The Doha Development Agenda Ten Years On: What Next?', in Rorden Wilkinson and James Scott (eds.), *Trade, Poverty, Development: Getting beyond the WTO's Doha Deadlock* (London: Routledge).

—(2014), 'Global Trade Governance', in Thomas G. Weiss and Rorden Wilkinson (eds.), *International Organization and Global Governance* (London: Routledge).

Hoekman, Bernard and Kostecki, Michel (1995), *The Political Economy of the World Trading System: From GATT to WTO* (Oxford: Oxford University Press).

Hoekman, Bernard and Mattoo, Aaditya (2007), 'Services, Economic Development and the Doha Round', in Donna Lee and Rorden Wilkinson (eds.), *The WTO after Hong Kong: Progress in, and Prospects for, the Doha Development Agenda* (London: Routledge).

Hoekman, Bernard and Mavroidis, Petros C. (2007), *The World Trade Organization: Law, Economics, Politics* (London: Routledge).

Hogan, Michael J. (1987), *The Marshall Plan* (Cambridge: Cambridge University Press).

Hook, Glenn D. (1984), 'The Nuclearization of Language: Nuclear Allergy as Political Metaphor', *Journal of Peace Research*, 21: 3.

Horn, Henrik and Mavroidis, Petros C. (2001), 'Economic and Legal Aspects of the Most-Favored-Nation Clause', *European Journal of Political Economy*, 17: 2 (June): 233–79.

Huang, Yasheng (2008), *Capitalism with Chinese Characteristics: Entrepreneurship and the State* (Cambridge: Cambridge University Press).

Huang, Zhixiong (2009), 'Rise and Fall of Trade Multilateralism: A Proposal for 'WTO à la carte' as an Alternative Approach for Trade Negotiations', paper presented to the Asian International Law Network Inaugural Conference, University of Tokyo, 3 August.

Hudec, Robert E. (1990), *The GATT Legal System and World Trade Diplomacy* (Salem, MA: Butterworth Legal Publishers), 2nd edn.

Hughes, Steve (1999), *International Labour Standards: The Formation and Development of an International Regime – New Zealand and the International Labour Organisation, 1919–1945*, unpublished PhD Thesis, University of Auckland, New Zealand.

Hughes, Steve and Haworth, Nigel (2010), *The International Labour Organisation: Coming in from the Cold* (London: Routledge).

Hughes, Steve and Wilkinson, Rorden (1998), 'International Labour Standards and World Trade: No Role for the World Trade Organisation?', *New Political Economy*, 3: 3 (November): 375–89.

Hulme, David (2010), *Global Poverty: How Global Governance is Failing the Poor* (London: Routledge).

Hulme, David and Turner, Oliver (2014), 'Poverty Reduction' in Thomas G. Weiss and Rorden Wilkinson (eds.), *International Organization and Global Governance* (London: Routledge).

Huntington, Samuel P. (1993), 'Why International Primacy Matters', *International Security*, 17: 4 (Spring): 68–83.

Hutton, Will (2007), *The Writing on the Wall: China and the West in the 21st Century* (London: Little, Brown).

Ibrahim, Tigani E. (1978), 'Developing Countries and the Tokyo Round', *Journal of World Trade Law*, 12: 1: 1–26.

ILO (1944), *Declaration of Philadelphia* (Montreal: ILO).

IMF (2013), *World Economic Outlook April 2013: Hopes, Realities, Risks* (Washington: IMF).

Irwin, Douglas A. (2001), 'Tariffs and Growth in Late Nineteenth Century America', *The World Economy*, 24: 1 (January): 15–30.

Ismail, Faizel (2009a), *Reforming the World Trade Organization: Developing Countries in the Doha Round* (Jaipur: CUTS/Friedrich Ebert Stiftung).

—(2009b), 'An Assessment of the WTO Doha Round, July–December 2008', *World Trade Review* 8: 4: 579–605.

—(2012), 'Is the Doha Round Dead? What is the Way Forward?', *World Economics*, 13: 3 (July–September): 143–69.

ITO Report (1947), *International Organization*, 1: 2 (June).

—(1950), *International Organization*, 4: 2 (May).

—(1951), *International Organization*, 5: 2 (May).

Jackson, John H. (1990a), *Restructuring the GATT System* (London: Pinter).

—. (1990b), 'Reflections on Restructuring the GATT', in Jeffrey J. Scott (ed.), *Completing the Uruguay Round* (Washington: Institute for International Economics).

Jackson, John H. (1993), 'A New Constitution for World Trade? Reforming the GATT System', in R. M. Stern (ed.), *The Multilateral Trading System* (Michigan: Michigan University Press).

Jackson, ohn H. (2000), The Jurisprudence of GATT and the WTO: insights on Treaty Law and Economic Relations

Jackson, Robert H. (1993), *Quasi States: Sovereignty, International Relations and the Third World* (Cambridge: Cambridge University Press).

Jacobson, Harold (1969), 'New States and Functional International Organisations: a Preliminary Report', in Robert Cox (ed.), *International Organisation: World Politics* (Basingstoke: Macmillan).

Jansen, Marion (2011), 'Internal Measures in the Multilateral Trading

System: Where are the Borders of the WTO Agenda?', in Thomas Cottier and Manfred Elsig (eds.), *Governing the World Trade Organization: Past, Present and Beyond Doha* (Cambridge: Cambridge University Press).

Jawara, Fatoumata and Kwa, Aileen (2003), *Behind the Scenes at the WTO: The Real World of International Trade Negotiations* (London: Zed Books).

Johnson, Harry G. (1968), 'US Economic Policy toward the Developing Countries', *Economic Development and Cultural Change*, 16: 3: 357–84.

Jolly, Richard, Emmerij, Louis and Weiss, Thomas G. (2009), *UN Ideas that Changed the World* (Bloomington: Indiana University Press).

Jones, Emily (2013), *Negotiating Against the Odds: A Guide for Trade Negotiators from Developing Countries* (London: Commonwealth Secretariat/Palgrave Macmillan).

Keohane, Robert O. (2002), *Power and Governance in a Partially Globalized World* (London: Routledge).

Keynes, John Maynard (1920), *The Economic Consequences of the Peace* (New York: Harcourt, Brace and Howe).

—(1946), 'The Balance of Payments of the United States', *Economic Journal*, 56: 222 (June): 172–87.

Kleimann, D. and Guinan, J. (2011), 'The Doha Round: An Obituary', *Global Governance Programme Policy Brief*, Robert Schuman Centre for Advanced Studies, European University Institute, No. 2011/1 (June), http://www.eui.eu/Projects/GGP/Documents/Publications/PolicyBriefs/PolicyBrief2011ifinal.pdf

Kock, Karin (1969), *International Trade Policy and the GATT, 1947–1967* (Stockholm: Almqvist and Wiksell).

Lakoff, George and Johnson, Mark (1980), 'The Metaphorical Structure of the Human Conceptual System', *Cognitive Science*, 4: 2 (April): 195–208.

Lall, K. B. (1965), Address to the 7th World Conference of the Society for International Development, Washington D. C. (March). Reprinted in WCSID, *International Development* (New York: WCSID).

Lamy, Pascal (2005), Speech to UNCTAD, Palais des Nations, Geneva (6 October). Available at http://www.wto.org/english/neww_e/sppl_e/spplo5_e.htm

—(2006), 'It's Time for a New "Geneva Consensus" on Making Trade Work for Development', Emile Noël lecture to New York University Law School, 30 October. Available at: http://www.wto.org/english/news_e/sppl_e/sppl45_e.htm

—(2009), Comments to the Closing Session of the WTO's 7th Ministerial Conference, 2 December.

—(2013), 'The Perilous Retreat from Global Trade Rules', *livemint*, 30 December 2013. Available at: http://www.livemint.com/Opin ion/5nq46BGZdXnvX6NXgjsy8I/The-perilous-retreat-from-global-tra de-rules--Pascal-Lamy.html

Lang, Andrew T. F. (2009), 'Legal Regimes and Regimes of Knowledge: Governing Global Services Trade', *LSE Legal Studies Working Paper*, No. 15.

Lanoszka, Anna (2001), 'The WTO Accession Process: Negotiating Participation in a Globalizing Economy', *Journal of World Trade*, 35: 4: 575–602.

Lawrence, Robert Z. (2006), 'Rulemaking Amidst Growing Diversity', *Journal of International Economic Law*, 9: 4.

Lee, Donna (2001), 'Endgame at the Kennedy Round: A Case Study of Multilateral Economic Diplomacy', *Diplomacy & Statecraft*, 12: 3 (September).

—(2013), 'Poverty and Cotton in the Doha Development Agenda', in Rorden Wilkinson and James Scott (eds.), *Trade, Poverty, Development: Getting Beyond the WTO's Doha Deadlock* (London: Routledge).

Lehmann, Jean-Pierre (2013), 'Bali Boost: WTO Lives, Snatched for Now From Jaws of Defeat', *YaleGlobal Online*, 10 December. Available at: http://yaleglobal.yale.edu/content/bali-boost-wto-lives-now-jaws-defeat

Li, Peilin (2011), 'China's New Stage of Development', *China: An International Journal*, 9: 1: 133–43.

Luce, Edward (2013), 'Obama Cannot Lead from Behind on Trade', *Financial Times*, 8 December.

Ludema, Rodney D. and Mayda, Anna Maria (2009), 'Do Countries Free Ride on MFN?', *Journal of International Economics*, 77: 2 (April): 137–50.

McGinnis, John O. and Movsesian, Mark L. (2004) 'Against Global Governance in the WTO', *Northwestern Public Law Research Paper*, no. 04-03, 28p.

Mack, Andrew J. R. (1975), 'Why Big Nations Lose Small Wars: The Politics of Asymmetric Conflict', *World Politics*, 27: 2 (January): 175–200.

McKenna, Barrie (2013), 'Trade-talk Gridlock Hinders Canada's Ability to Take Care of Business', *The Globe and Mail*, 30 June.

McRae, D. M. and Thomas, J. C. (1983), 'The GATT and Multilateral Treaty Making: The Tokyo Round', *American Journal of International Law*, 77: 1 (January): 51–83.

Mandela, Nelson (1998), Statement on the 50th Anniversary of the Multilateral Trading System, Geneva, 19 May WT/FIFTY/H/ST/13

Mansfield, Mike (1989), 'The US and Japan: Sharing our Destinies', *Foreign Affairs*, 68: 2 (Spring): 3–15.

Maswood, Javed and Crump, Larry (2007), 'Introduction', in Larry Crump and S. Javed Maswood (eds.), *Developing Countries and Global Trade Negotiations* (London: Routledge).

Mavroidis, Petros C. (2011), 'Doha, Dohalf, Dohaha? The WTO Licks its Wounds', *Trade, Law, and Development*, 3: 2 (Fall): 367–81.

Mazower, Mark (2012), *Governing the World: The History of an Idea* (London: Penguin).

Meléndez-Ortiz, Ricardo, Bellman, Christophe and Mendoza, Miguel Rodriguez (eds.) (2012), *The Future and the WTO: Confronting the challenges* (Geneva: ICTSD).

Michalopoulos, Constantine (1999), 'Developing Countries' Participation in the World Trade Organization', *World Bank Policy Research Working Papers*, No. 1906.

Milward, Alan S. (1979), *War, Economy and Society, 1939–1945* (Berkeley: University of California Press).

Momani, Bessma (2010), 'IMF Rhetoric on Reducing Poverty and Inequality', in Jennifer Clapp and Rorden Wilkinson (eds.), *Global Governance, Poverty and Inequality* (London: Routledge).

Moore, Mike (2003) *A World without Walls: Freedom, Development, Free Trade and Global Governance* (Cambridge: Cambridge University Press).

Murphy, Craig N. (1994), *International Organization and Industrial Change: Global Governance since 1850* (Cambridge: Polity).

—(1999), 'Inequality, Turmoil and Democracy: Global Political-Economic Visions at the End of the Century', *New Political Economy*, 4: 2: 289–304.

—(2006), *The United Nations Development Programme: A Better Way?* (Cambridge: Cambridge University Press).

—(2012), 'Lessons to be Learned from the Challenges to Achieving the MDGs in Africa', in Rorden Wilkinson and David Hulme (eds.), *The Millennium Development Goals and Beyond: Global Development after 2015* (London: Routledge).

Narlikar, Amrita (2003), *International Trade and Developing Countries: Bargaining Together in the GATT and WTO* (London: Routledge).

Narlikar, Amrita and Tussie, Diana (2004), 'The G20 at the Cancun Ministerial: Developing Countries and their Evolving Coalitions in the WTO', *World Economy*, 27: 7 (July): 947–66.

Narlikar, Amrita and Wilkinson, Rorden (2004), 'Collapse at the WTO: A Cancún Post-Mortem', *Third World Quarterly*, 25: 3 (April): 447–60.

O'Brien, Robert (2013) 'Review of Steve Hughes and Nigel Haworth's "The

International Labour Organisation (ILO): Coming in From the Cold"', *Global Labour Journal*, 4: 2: 152–4.

OECD (2012), 'A New Narrative for World Trade', *OECD Observer*, No. 290–1. Available at: http://www.oecdobserver.org/news/fullstory.php/aid/3785/A_new_narrative_for_world_trade.html

Orwell, George ([1946] 1962), 'Politics and the English Language', reprinted in *Inside the Whale and Other Essays* (London: Penguin).

—(1946), 'In Front of Your Nose', *Tribune*, 22 March.

Ostry, Sylvia (1997), *The Post-Cold War Trading System* (London: University of Chicago Press).

—(2007), 'Trade, Development and the Doha Development Agenda', in Donna Lee and Rorden Wilkinson (eds.), *The WTO after Hong Kong: Progress in, and prospects for, the Doha Development Agenda* (London: Routledge, 2007).

Oxfam GB (2000), 'Institutional Reform of the WTO', *Discussion Paper* (March).

Oyane, Satoshi (2001), '"Plurilateralism" of the United States and its APEC Policies', *IDE APEC Study Center Working Paper*, No. 00/01 – 5 (March).

Panagariya, Arvind (1999), 'On the "Extravagant" Predictions of Benefit from the Uruguay Round', *The Economic Times*, 25 August.

Patterson, Gardner (1966), *Discrimination in International Trade: The Policy Issues 1945–1965* (Princeton: Princeton University Press).

Payne, Anthony J. (2005), *The Global Politics of Unequal Development* (Basingstoke: Palgrave).

Peet, Richard (2009), *Unholy Trinity: The IMF, World Bank and WTO* (London: Zed books), 2nd edn.

Peña, Alejandro Milcíades and David, Thomas Richard (2013), 'Globalisation from Above? Corporate Social Responsibility, the Workers' Party and the Origins of the World Social Forum', *New Political Economy*, available on early view: http://dx.doi.org/10.1080/13563467.2013.779651

People's Daily (2010), 'China's Status as Developing Nation Beyond Doubt', 11 August.

Phelan, Edward (1946), 'The ILO and the United Nations: The Director-General's Address to the Assembly', *International Labour Review*, 54: 5–6 (November-December): 281–4.

Pilling, David (2011), 'Trans-Pacific Partnership: Far-Reaching Agreement Could Form Powerful New Bloc', *Financial Times*, 8 November.

Pogge, Thomas (2008), *World Poverty and Human Rights* (Cambridge: Polity), 2nd edn.

—(2010), *Politics as Usual: What Lies Behind the Pro-Poor Rhetoric* (Cambridge: Polity).

Rodrik, Dani (2011), *The Globalization Paradox: Why Global Markets, States and Democracy Can't Coexist* (Oxford: Oxford University Press).

Rooth, Tim (1999), 'Britain's Other Dollar Problem: Economic Relations with Canada, 1945–1950', *Journal of Imperial and Commonwealth History*, 27: 1 (January): 81–108.

Rose, Andrew K. (2004), 'Do We Really Know that the WTO Increases Trade?', *American Economic Review*, 94: 1: 98–114.

Saner, Raymond (2012), 'Plurilateral Agreements: Key to Solving Impasse of WTO/Doha Round and Basis for Future Trade Agreements within the WTO Context', *CSEND Policy Brief*, No. 7 (April).

Sampson, Gary P. (2004), 'Is there a Need for Restructuring the Collaboration Among the WTO and UN Agencies so as to Harness Their Complementarities?', *Journal of International Economic Law*, 7: 3: 717–27.

Schwab, Susan (2009), 'Reflections on Trade Policy', speech given at the University of Manchester, 20 May.

—(2011), 'After Doha', *Foreign Affairs*, 90: 3 (May/June): 104–17.

Scott, James (2008), 'The Uses and Misuses of Trade Negotiation Simulations', *Journal of World Trade*, 42: 1: 87–103.

Scott, James (2010), 'Developing Countries in the ITO and GATT Negotiations', *Journal of International Trade Law and Policy*, 9: 1: 5-24.

Scott, James and Harman, Sophie (2013), 'Beyond TRIPs: Why the WTO's Doha Round is Unhealthy', *Third World Quarterly*, 34: 8: 1361–76.

Scott, James and Wilkinson, Rorden (2010), 'What Happened to Doha in Geneva? Re-engineering the WTO's Image While Missing Key Opportunities', *European Journal of Development Research*, 22: 2 (April): 141–53.

—(2011), 'The Poverty of the Doha Round and the Least Developed Countries', *Third World Quarterly*, 32: 4 (May): 611–27.

—(2012), 'The Politics and Perils of Plurilaterals', *Economic and Political Weekly*, 47: 43 (27 October): 16–19.

—(2013a), 'China Threat? Evidence from the WTO', *Journal of World Trade*, 47: 4 (August): 761–82.

—(2013b), 'The Promise of "Development" and the Doha Development Agenda' in Rorden Wilkinson and James Scott (eds.), *Trade, Poverty, Development: Getting beyond the WTO's Doha Deadlock* (London: Routledge).

Sell, Susan (2014), 'Global Economic Governance: Intellectual Property', in Moschella, Manuela and Weaver, Catherine (eds.), *Handbook of Global Economic Governance* (London: Routledge).

Shiva, Vandana ([2000] 2006), 'War Against Nature and the People of the South', in Della Giusta, Marina, Kambhampati, Uma S., Wade, Robert H. (eds.), *Critical Perspectives On Globalization* (Cheltenham: Edward Elgar).

Siles-Brügge, Gabriel (2013), 'Explaining the Resilience of Free Trade: The Smoot-Hawley Myth and the Crisis', *Review of International Political Economy*, early view available at: http://www.tandfonline.com/doi/full/1 0.1080/09692290.2013.830979#.Um-RA2xFA5s

Singer, Peter (2004), *One World: The Ethics of Globalization* (New Haven: Yale University Press), 2nd edn.

Smith, J. Russell (1919), 'Trade and a League of Nations or Economic Internationalism', *Annals of the American Academy of Political and Social Science*, 83 (May): 287–305.

Solinger, Dorothy J. (2003), 'Chinese Urban Jobs and the WTO', *The China Journal*, 49: 61–87.

Sontag, Susan (2002), *Illness as Metaphor and AIDS and Its Metaphors* (London: Penguin Books).

Srinivasan, Thirukodikaval N. (1998), *Developing Countries and the Multilateral Trading System* (Boulder, Colorado and Oxford: Westview).

Stanley, Alessandra and Hoge, Warren (2001), 'Protestors at Bay, Rich Nations' Chiefs to Meet in Genoa', *New York Times*, 18 July.

Steger, Debra P. (2009), 'The Future of the WTO: The Case for Institutional Reform', *Journal of International Economic Law*, 12: 4: 803–33.

Stettinius, Edward R. (1944), *Lend-Lease: Weapon for Victory* (London: Penguin).

Stiglitz, Joseph and Charlton, Andrew (2013), *The Right to Trade: Rethinking the Aid for Trade Agenda* (London: Commonwealth Secretariat). Available at: https://publications.thecommonwealth.org/the-right-to-trade-997–5p.aspx

Sutherland Report (Report of the Consultative Board of the Director-General Supachai Panitchpakdi) (2004), *The Future of the WTO* (Geneva: World Trade Organisation). Available at: www.wto.org/english/thewto_e/10anniv_e/future_wto_e.pdf

Teivainen, Teivo (2002), 'The World Social Forum and Global Democratisation: Learning from Porto Alegre', *Third World Quarterly*, 23: 4: 621–32.

Thelen, Kathleen and Steinmo, Sven (1992), 'Historical Institutionalism in Comparative Politics', in Sven Steinmo, Kathleen Thelen and Frank

Longstreth (eds.), *Structuring Politics: Historical Institutionalism in Comparative Analysis* (Cambridge: Cambridge University Press).

Thérien, Jean-Philippe (2005), 'Beyond the North–South Divide: The Two Tales of World Poverty', in Rorden Wilkinson (ed.), *The Global Governance Reader* (London: Routledge).

Thomas, P. Singh, Sukhpal, Kanitkar, Ajit, Ahmed, Sara and Johnson, E. Michael (1994), 'Dunkel Text: Implications for Rural Sector', *Economic and Political Weekly*, 29: 13 (26 March): A42–A52.

Tijmes-Lhl, Jaime (2009), 'Consensus and Majority Voting in the WTO', *World Trade Review*, 8: 3 (July): 417–37.

Turner, Oliver (2009), 'China's Recovery: Why the Writing Was Always on the Wall', *Political Quarterly*, 80: 1 (January/March): 111–18.

—(2013), ''Finishing the Job': the UN Special Committee on Decolonization and the Politics of Self-Government', *Third World Quarterly*, 34: 7: 1193–208.

Tussie, Diana (ed.) (2009), *The Politics of Trade: The Role of Research in Trade Policy and Negotiation* (Dordrecht: Brill).

UNCTAD (2001), *WTO Accessions and Development Policies* (New York and Geneva: UNCTAD).

UNCTE (1948), *Final Act of the United Nations Conference on Trade and Employment* (New York: Interim Commission for the International Trade Organization).

US Department of State (1945), Proposals for Expansion of World Trade and Employment (Washington: Department of State).

van Dormael, Armand (1978), *Bretton Woods: Birth of a Monetary System* (Basingstoke: Macmillan).

VanGrasstek, Craig (2013), *The History and Future of the World Trade Organization* (Geneva: WTO).

Viner, Jacob (1947), 'Conflicts of Principle in Drafting a Trade Charter', *Foreign Affairs*, 25: 4 (July).

Wade, Robert (2001), 'Showdown at the World Bank', *New Left Review*, 7 (January-February): 124–37.

—(2003), 'What Strategies are Viable for Developing Countries Today? The World Trade Organization and the Shrinking of "Development Space"', *Review of International Political Economy*, 10: 4 (November).

—(2010), 'After the Crisis: Industrial Policy and the Developmental State in Low-Income Countries', *Global Policy*, 1: 2: 150–61.

Wallach, Lori and Woodall, Patrick 92004), *Whose Trade Organization?* (New York: The New Press).

Wang, Shaoguang (2000), 'The Social and Political Implications of

China's WTO Membership', *Journal of Contemporary China*, 9: 25: 373–405.

Warwick Commission (2007), *The Multilateral Trade Regime: Which Way Forward?* (Coventry: University of Warwick).

Weaver, Catherine (2010), 'Reforming the World Bank', in Jennifer Clapp and Rorden Wilkinson (eds.), *Global Governance, Poverty and Inequality* (London: Routledge).

Weiss, Thomas G. (2003), 'The Illusion of UN Security Council Reform', *The Washington Quarterly*, 26: 4: 147–61.

—(2009), *What's Wrong with the United Nations and How to Fix it* (Cambridge: Polity).

—(2012a), 'ECOSOC and the MDGs: What Can Be Done?' in Rorden Wilkinson and David Hulme (eds.), *The Millennium Development Goals and Beyond: Global Development after 2015* (London: Routledge).

—(2012b), *What's Wrong with the United Nations and How to Fix it* (Cambridge: Polity), 2nd edn.

Weiss, Thomas G. and Wilkinson, Rorden (2014), 'Rethinking Global Governance? Complexity, Authority, Power and Change', *International Studies Quarterly*, 58: 2 (March): 207–15.

Whalley, John (2000), 'What Can the Developing Countries Infer from the Uruguay Round Models for Future Negotiation', *Policy Series in International Trade and Commodities*, No. 4 (Geneva: UNCTAD). Available at: http://unctad.org/en/Docs/itcdtab6_en.pdf

WHO (1946), *Constitution of the World Health Organization* (New York: United Nations).

Wilcox, Clair (1949a), *A Charter for World Trade* (London and New York: Macmillan).

—(1949b), 'The Promise of the World Trade Charter', *Foreign Affairs*, 27: 3 (April).

Wilkinson, Rorden (1999), 'Labour and Trade-Related Regulation: Beyond the Trade/Labour Standards Debate?', *British Journal of Politics and International Relations*, 1: 2 (June): 165–91.

—(2000), *Multilateralism and the World Trade Organisation: The Architecture and Extension of International Trade Regulation* (London: Routledge).

—(2002), 'Peripheralising Labour: The ILO, WTO and the Completion of the Bretton Woods Project', in Jeffrey Harrod and Robert O'Brien (eds.), *Global Unions? Theory and Strategies of Organized Labour in the Global Political Economy* (London: Routledge).

—(2003) 'ACUNS in Cancún', *ACUNS Informational Memorandum*, 57 (Fall): 6–8.

—(2005a), 'Managing Global Civil Society: the WTO's Engagement with NGOs', in Randall Germain and Michael Kenny (eds.), *The Idea of Global Civil Society: Politics and Ethics in a Globalising Era* (London: Routledge), pp. 156–74.

—(2005b), 'The World Trade Organisation and the Regulation of International Trade', in Wyn Grant and Dominic Kelly (eds.), *The Politics of International Trade: Actors, Issues, Regions* (Basingstoke: Palgrave), pp. 13–29.

—(2006a), *The WTO: Crisis and the Governance of Global Trade* (London: Routledge).

—(2006b), 'A Ghost of a Chance: ACUNS in Hong Kong', *ACUNS Informational Memorandum*, 65 (Winter): 1– 3.

—(2006c), 'The WTO in Hong Kong: What it Really Means for the Doha Development Agenda', *New Political Economy*, 11: 2 (June): 291– 303.

—(2008), 'Family Dramas: Politics, Diplomacy and Governance in the WTO', in Andrew F. Cooper, Brian Hocking and William Maley (eds.), *Global Governance and Diplomacy: Worlds Apart?* (New York: Palgrave), pp. 164–79.

—(2009), 'Language, Power and Multilateral Trade Negotiations', *Review of International Political Economy*, 16: 4 (October): 597–619.

—(2011), 'Measuring the WTO's Performance: An Alternative Account', *Global Policy*, 2: 1 (January): 43–52.

—(2012), 'Of Butchery and Bicycles: The WTO and the "Death" of the Doha Development Agenda', *Political Quarterly*, 83: 2 (April-June): 395–401.

—(2014), '*Plus ça change?* Business as Usual in the Governance of Global Trade', in Moschella, Manuela and Weaver, Catherine (eds.), *Handbook of Global Economic Governance* (London: Routledge).

Wilkinson, Rorden, Hannah, Erin and Scott, James (2014), 'The WTO in Bali: What MC9 Means for the Doha Development Agenda and Why It Matters', *Third World Quarterly*, 35: 6 (July 2014).

Wilkinson, Rorden and Hulme, David (eds.) (2012), *The Millennium Development Goals and Beyond: Global Development after 2015* (London: Routledge).

Wilkinson, Rorden and Scott, James (2008), 'Developing Country Participation in the GATT: A Reassessment', *World Trade Review*, 7: 3 (July): 473–510.

Winham, Gilbert R. (2006), 'An Institutional Theory of WTO Decision-Making: Why Negotiation in the WTO resembles Law-Making in the US

Congress', *Controversies in Global Politics and Societies Occasional Paper*, Munk Centre for International Studies, University of Toronto, No. II.

Winters, L. Alan (1990), 'The Road to Uruguay', *The Economic Journal*, 100: 403 (December).

Wolf, Martin (2013), 'The Future of Global Trade Policy', CUTS 30th Anniversary Lecture, Commonwealth Secretariat, Marlborough House, London, 15 July.

Wolfe, Robert (2014), 'Does Sunshine Make a Difference: How Transparency Brings the Trading System to Life', in Moschella, Manuela and Weaver, Catherine (eds.), *Handbook of Global Economic Governance* (London: Routledge).

World Bank (2013), *FY14 World Bank Budget* (Washington: World Bank). Available at: http://www-wds.worldbank.org/external/default/ WDSContentServer/WDSP/IB/2013/08/13/000452162_20130813122 542/Rendered/PDF/781750BR0R2013000PUBLIC00Box379801B.pdf

WTO (1994), *Agreement Establishing the World Trade Organization* (GATT: Geneva).

—(1999a), 'WTO Organizes "Geneva Week" for Non-Resident Delegations', *WTO Press Release*, no. 141 (26 October).

—(1999b), 'Labour Issue Is "False Debate", Obscures Underlying Consensus, WTO Chief Mike Moore Tells Unions', *WTO Press Release*, no. 152 (28 November).

—(2001a), Doha Ministerial Declaration, WT/MIN(01)/DEC/1, 20 November.

—(2001b), Decision on Implementation-Related Issues and Concerns, WT/MIN(01)/17, 20 November.

—(2001c), Declaration on the TRIPs Agreement and Public Health, WT/ MIN(01)/DEC/2, 20 November.

—(2002), 'Moore Stresses Development Role at WTO', *Press Release*, No. 290 (29 April).

—(2004), 'Doha Work Programme: Decision adopted by the General Council on 1 August 2004', WT/L/579, 2 August.

—(2005), Hong Kong Ministerial Declaration, adopted 18 December WT/ MIN(05)/W/3/Rev.2.

—(2012a), *International Trade Statistics* (Geneva: WTO Statistics Division).

—(2012b), 'WTO Membership Rises to 157 with Entry of Russia and Vanuatu', *Press Release*, No. 671 (22 August).

—(2012c), 'WTO and OECD to Develop Statistics on Trade in Value Added', *WTO News Item* (15 March). Available at: http://www.wto.org/ english/news_e/news12_e/miwi_15mar12_e.htm

—(2013a), 'Azevêdo Sends Letter Asking Ministers for "Personal, Active Engagement" ahead of Bali', *WTO News Item*, 30 September. Available at: http://www.wto.org/english/news_e/news13_e/tnc_infstat_30sep13_e. htm

—(2013b), 'USTR Froman Warns Poor Countries Would Be the Biggest Losers If Bali Fails', *WTO News Items*, 1 October: available at: http://www.wto.org/english/news_e/news13_e/pfor_01oct13_e.htm

—(2013c), *International Trade Statistics* (Geneva: WTO Statistics Division).

Yusuf, Abdulqawi A. (1980), '"Differential and More Favourable Treatment": The GATT Enabling Clause', *Journal of World Trade Law*, 14: 6: 488–507.

Zartman, I. William, and Rubin, Jeffrey (2002), 'The Study of Power and the Practice of Negotiation', in Zartman, I. William and Rubin, Jeffrey (eds.), *Power and Negotiation* (Ann Arbor: University of Michigan Press).

Zeng, Ka (2013), 'Legal Capacity and Developing Country Performance in the Panel Stage of the WTO Dispute Settlement System', *Journal of World Trade*, 47: 1 (February): 187–213.

Index